Copyright © 2021 Zoe Lambreas

All images belong to the author, are out of copyright or are used by permission.

Editing: Zoe Lambreas
Typographic Design: Zoe Lambreas

All rights reserved. No part of this publication may be reproduced, stored in a retrieval system, or transmitted in any form or by any means-for example, electronic, photocopy, recording-without the prior written permission of the author. The only exception is brief quotations in printed reviews.

ISBN: 978-0-9946333-1-6

Second edition: February 2022, Melbourne

Cover photograph shows Theo and Argyro with baby Voula. The background is a typical rural scene around the Western District and Hamilton.

A WALK IN MY SKIN

(the ~~mis~~Adventures of Aussie Kids with Migrant Parents)

Zoe Lambreas

Acknowledgment

I would like to thank each of my dear family and friends who kindly obliged me by spending precious time recording the chapters, so that a simplified audio version of this book, *Speak English Like Australians!*, is available on YouTube for learners of English. Your contributions are greatly appreciated. For more information please go to: *www.speaklikeaustralians.com*

A special thank you to my wonderful husband for his unfailing encouragement over the years.

Thank you also to my colleagues who supported me and made suggestions.

Zoe Lambreas

Dedication

This book is dedicated to my beloved parents, Argyro and Theo, whose courage and desire for a better life propelled them, like so many others, to come to Australia in search of a better life; on whose labour this land depended for its prosperity and development. In exchange for their toil, Australia did indeed become "the land of plenty" and God has wonderfully blessed them.

Of course and especially for my brothers, Peter and Jim, who provided so many memories for the anecdotes in this book!

Zoe Lambreas

the town of Hamilton in 1881

State Library of Victoria
http://handle.slv.vic.gov.au/10381/257676

sheep country: The green and gold colours of Australia are a natural part of typical rural scenes, on the outskirts of Hamilton.

Contents

Characters in the book		ii
Chapter 1	A Migrant to Australia	1
Chapter 2	Assimilation	8
Chapter 3	The Marriage Proposal	12
Chapter 4	Family	23
Chapter 5	School	28
Chapter 6	School Ceremonies and Rituals	32
Chapter 7	Imperial Australia	38
Chapter 8	ANZAC Day	50
Chapter 9	Katie and The Beatles	54
Chapter 10	Music	60
Chapter 11	The Accident	68
Chapter 12	Celebrations	76
Chapter 13	Fun, Games and Pets	84
Chapter 14	At Home	92
Chapter 15	Obsessions and Hobbies	98
Chapter 16	The Woodshed	104
Chapter 17	The Hamilton Show	108
Chapter 18	Going for Sunday Drives	114
Chapter 19	Guy Fawkes Night	118
Chapter 20	Pets	122
Chapter 21	The Billy-Cart	132
Chapter 22	The Monorail	138
Chapter 23	Sticks and Stones	142
Chapter 24	The Pipe Tunnel and Prince	148
Chapter 25	The Bike	154
Chapter 26	The Bicycle Lesson	160
Chapter 27	The Childhood Home	164
Chapter 28	The First School Day Every Year	170
Chapter 29	Pleasures	174
Chapter 30	The Club	180
Chapter 31	The Sleepover	186
Chapter 32	New Beginnings	191

Voula, Jimmy and Peter in the Hamilton Botanical Gardens (circa 1967)

Characters in the book

Theo is a migrant from Greece who arrived in Australia in 1953 and married Argyro in early 1956. He became the business partner of Andy Hadis.

Andy Hadis is the original owner of Lucas Cafe which operated from 1951 to 1969. He married Katina and they had four children: Theo, Peggy, Steven and John.

Voula is the daughter of Theo and Argyro while Peter is the older son and Jimmy is the "baby".

Bob Tydon is Peter's best friend and lives across the road from Pete. He's a keen *Bombers* supporter and owns and breeds about fifty pigeons.

Don and Margaret Shmitz are neighbours of Theo and Argyro with three kids of their own.

Chapter 1
A Migrant to Australia

Theodoros, being the eldest son, keenly felt the responsibility of supporting his widowed mother and five siblings. Ever since his twentieth year he had shouldered this burden, when his father had drowned in the Messenian Gulf, trying to save his two grandchildren after the overladen boat they were travelling in, had overturned. He was returning his grandchildren to their parents in Kalamata, where he had sent Theo and his youngest son, George, to help out in their sister's bakery. Kalamata was a safe haven from the civil unrest and roaming militia who captured country folk at random. After the accident, the body of Theo's father was never recovered. However, the corpses of the two children were lifted out of the sea and placed on a wooden, horse-drawn cart for their final journey home to their parents. Theo was there when the cart arrived outside the bakery and he shared the pain and anguish of his distraught sister, Panayiota, and brother-in-law, Stavros. The grief of Stavros was so intense that he suffered a break-down and lost touch with reality. Sadly, Stavros never recovered and was institutionalised for the remainder of his life. It fell to his wife and older daughter to earn enough money in the bakery to pay for his care.

And it fell upon Theo to seek means to nurture his mother and siblings, but then, ominously, the Second World War struck

Europe. Seeking a viable future, gave way to the need for survival in an impoverished Greece, devastated by the War, when German and Italian soldiers occupied Greece and destroyed the country's infrastructure. City dwellers, like the Athenians, had starved to death while villagers were forced to surrender their livestock and produce to hungry, wandering enemy soldiers. Then, after World War II, the unthinkable happened when Greece became embroiled in a vicious civil war from 1946 to 1949, dividing friends, neighbours and even brothers, who struggled with right and left ideologies, backed on one side by the UK and the USA and on the other by Albania, Yugoslavia, Bulgaria and the Soviet Union. This civil war was horrific and many Greeks killed each other, before the communist left was defeated by the Hellenic Army.

After these wars Greece was ravaged and needed strong, skillful leadership, but the federal government had little power and from 1949 to 1953 there were nine different governing leaders, each holding tenure in office from several days to less than 2 years. Theo had survived as a prisoner during the civil war and now, in such politically restless days, desperately sought a way to help his family. Of course he felt fortunate and blessed when he secured a job as a policeman in Athens!

At that time, the youth of Athens were often seen wearing jumpers or jackets with one sleeve unworn and left dangling: for some reason it had become a fashion fad, or perhaps it was a political protest against the ruling government of the day. The Greek Government responded by issuing policemen with scissors to snip off the sleeves left hanging loose and unworn. After all his struggles during the wars, Theo found this initiative somewhat amusing: it found a resonant chord with his humour.

Another government determination was to enforce strict food and hygiene laws for cafes and restaurants to "lift" the standard of living. Therefore, much of the police work involved the inspection and strict implementation of these laws. Proprietors of food businesses were given only one warning by a white-gloved police officer, who had detected any dust whatsoever, on their premises. If dust was observed on a subsequent visit, the business had to be permanently shut-down by the police. This was Theo's job, but he abhorred the draconian and excessive aspect of this part of his work! To put someone's livelihood in jeopardy, by being the means of enforcing rigid and extreme government policies, was beyond his sense of justice. Although his job was easy and well-paid, Theo lived by the dictates of his conscience. If he was to be the instrument by which others were ruined thus unfairly, he would rather suffer himself. He quit his job! Now what would he do?

By this time, 1953, Theo was in his early thirties, six feet four inches tall, handsome and full of hope for the future. What could he turn his hand to? He had helped his two unmarried sisters by providing them with their own stone houses as part of their dowries, but now there remained the provision for his two younger brothers. He knew the olive groves they had inherited from their father, could not sustain all three of them should they each marry and receive a third portion. He was egalitarian towards his brothers and finally persuaded himself to take drastic measures. After much heart-searching, Theodoros decided to leave Greece for a chance at a better life overseas, in Australia. His brothers would then be able to eke out a feasible living from their inheritance, splitting the family farmland in half, rather than three ways.

Like many others, Theo thought he would make lots of money and send some back to his beleaguered family in Greece. Of course cash in envelopes is not secure, but this was a common practice. Indeed for several years, he posted cash to his brother Panayiotis. Who knows if he actually received it?

Thus it was that in October 1953, he boarded the ship, Fairstar, bound for Melbourne. That year, Theo was one of approximately 75,000 new migrants who came, with high hopes, to settle in Australia. He emigrated with the support of the Australian Government for whom he worked for two years to repay his fare to Australia. Nothing for nothing: there is always a catch, so he was obligated to work at whatever the government determined, in order to gradually repay his debt, through a small deduction from his wages. That was the deal, known as the Assisted Passage Programme and migrants were brought over to build Australia's infrastructure: it was physically demanding and often back-breaking work.

Theo was settled in Bonegilla, where migrants were given a couple of weeks of accommodation. It is located about 300 km north-east of Melbourne. He indeed remained there for two weeks learning basic English, until he was allocated work, laying railway tracks in Victoria.

When Theo first started this job he worked hard, because being grateful, young and strong he wanted to impress his new workmates. However, his crew of co-workers, who were all Aussies, told him to take it easy. "Just relax a little matey," they told him. "There's no hurry. She'll be right!" That was Theo's first experience of the enigmatic Australian culture of "taking it easy" and "she'll be right mate". Theo soon learnt what it meant to have a tea-break or when it was time for a "smoko".

Regardless of these work breaks, Theo's job was hard, physical and critical to the framework and facilities of a young Australia.

His next job was to strip the bark off trees in Western Australia. Back then, Australia had a large tannin industry which depended on harvesting Black Wattle trees in the bush. The bark was used mainly by tanneries, for tanning leather, but was also used for making ropes and nets. The left-over bark was called tanbark and was used as mulch or as a covering for paths. In fact *The Tan*, the 4 km path around the Royal Botanic Gardens in Melbourne, received its name because it was originally spread with tan bark.

When Theo's two years of government work was up, he returned to Melbourne. He was at his wit's end as to what to do. What would you do? As he had worked on building railway tracks, Theo decided to take a train to "the end of the line", to a place he had become accustomed to whilst working in Victoria. The railway track ended at Hamilton, in the Western District. Having been there during his work details, he had become familiar with this town, which was quite large, having a population of around 11,000. Hamilton is a rural community and was famous for its Merino sheep farms. Australia's 22nd Prime Minister, Mr Malcolm Fraser had a farm there, Nareen. The town has two main streets of shops: in Gray Street and in Thompson Street. Theo disembarked the train and walked till he got to Thompson Street.

While working alongside Aussies, Theo had learnt to drink a glass or two of beer rather than "retsina", the Greek wine, which has been made for at least 2,000 years. When he spied a pub, the Commercial Hotel, he decided to go in for a beer. It felt good to be off the train and to sit in a cool place alongside other men, even though he didn't know anyone. It might interest you to know that in those days it was illegal for women to drink in a pub: it was men only!

While he was drinking his schooner, he looked up and saw a man wink at him. Theo was immediately offended and became angry. He felt the blood rush to his face, because in Greece, men only winked at women. Theo didn't want anyone to have any wrong ideas about him, so feeling the insult very deeply, he jumped up, went over, and angrily grabbed the man's collar. Wanting to defend his honour, he reached backwards with his free hand making a fist, but it was grabbed from behind by a couple of blokes, who fortunately, sat nearby. They pulled Theo away and asked him why he wanted to fight. In his broken English he explained that the man had winked at him and that it was an insult to his manhood! The other men explained that in Australia, a wink can sometimes mean "G' day" or "How ya goin' mate?"

Theo felt humiliated, but was soon able to smile with the other men round about and shake hands with the unfortunate one who had winked at him. It had all been a cultural misunderstanding, but it became apparent to Theo that Australia had some very strange customs! As he left the pub he heard a racial slur that had become familiar to his ears, "Bloody dago!" and then the roar of laughter. His face crimsoned again. Theo left the pub ashamed of himself and shaking his head in wonder. Australia certainly would take some getting used to; even after two years he still felt alienated. It is true that through ignorance we make mistakes, and by mistakes we can also learn. However, would he ever learn? Unfortunately, Theo thought he had heard "How ya goin' Mike?" Following this incident, and for the rest of his life, Theo usually greeted people with a wink and "How ya goin *Mike*?" rather than "mate". He wanted to be friendly and remembered his lesson well. As sometimes happens with learners of another language, Theo just had not differentiated between the two words. His future family never corrected him. They thought it was his own private joke!

Theo arrived in Australia carrying only his passport, this small suitcase and a bit of cash, half of which he kindly gave to a 19-year-old, Greek passenger from Kalamata. This enterprising teenager later opened a jewellery shop: Alex Brothers, in Lonsdale Street, Melbourne.

Landing: Passengers disembark at Port Melbourne in 1954 *The Sydney Morning Herald*

Trains left from Station Pier taking migrants to a number of migrant camps, including Bonegilla. (1950)
http://discover.bonegilla.org.au/

Block 4 of the Bonegilla camp while operational in 1954 (one of 30 Migrant Hostels operating in Australia at the time.)

English lessons at Bathurst Migrant Camp (1951)
National Archives of Australia

Chapter 2
Assimilation

Theo left the pub humbled and shaking his head. Australia certainly was a weird place! People had different ways of doing things! Not only that, but Mediterranean food like olives and feta cheese were unavailable in the local shops! In 1953 there was no idea of multiculturalism and migrants were expected to assimilate into the Anglo-Saxon culture prevalent in Australia. Would he ever fit in? He felt vulnerable, knowing that Aussie customs could take him by surprise when he least expected it, as had happened in the pub. All it had taken was a wink to put him off-balance and uncertain of himself. He determined to work hard to establish himself in this great land of opportunity.

As Theo walked down Gray Street, the main street, he heard his tummy rumble and realised he was feeling hungry. It was then he noticed the "Lucas Cafe" sign. What he did not see at the time was that there was a Greek flag flying over the shop!

Anyway, a nice smell drifted from the doorway. Theo was familiar now with the smell of "chips" and decided it would be a good idea to buy some. Inside, the shop was long and cool, and there were tables and chairs filling up most of the space. At the front, beside the door was a counter. Theo could see there were ice-creams, lollies, chocolates and cigarettes for sale. From behind the counter stood a man regarding him with interest.

"Chips plis," requested Theo. The man smiled at Theo's accent and asked where he was from. After introducing themselves, they got to know a bit more about each other. Andy, was the owner of Lucas Cafe and he was a Greek from Cyprus, then a British colony. His English was pretty good, because he had learnt the language in Cyprus as a young child. Anyway, to Theo, Andy's English was as advanced as Shakespeare's! While they talked, Theo told him he needed a job. As it happened, Andy obliged and offered Theo employment, as a much needed kitchen hand.

After a few months, Theo was chopping potatoes and grilling steaks like an expert! The following year, Andy's two Cypriot business partners left Hamilton for Melbourne. When this happened Theo offered himself as a partner and a part-owner of the business. They decided that Andy, who spoke English well would be the front man, while Theo would do most of the cooking and cleaning out the back. This arrangement was good for business but not for the improvement of Theo's English.

That is how Andy Hadis and Theo became business partners. The two men worked well together and the partnership extended to fifteen years, when the business closed its doors. Over time, the cafe became very busy and Theo was obliged to work long hours: from 7 or 8am until 8 or 9pm. Being a partner did not obviate him from labouring tasks. On the contrary, by the time he had cleaned up and locked up the shop, he sometimes didn't get home till 10pm! Theo always walked home, about 900 metres. Anyway he didn't have a driver's licence and the cool night air felt refreshing, after being indoors all day. Theo lodged with Andy and his small family in French Street across the road from the Botanical Gardens.

Although Theo was doing well in his new country, and trying to assimilate to the Aussie culture, he felt something was lacking!

He did not feel quite right! He found himself thinking about a lovely girl, Argyro, whom he had known in Greece. They had only spoken three or four times, the first time at the 3-year-memorial service of her mother's brother. Theo had served under *The Captain*, otherwise known as *The Eagle of Mani*, and had loved and admired him. Unfortunately, during the civil war following the Second World War, Captain Panos had been shot and killed by guerrillas in 1947. Argyro never got over his death, which spiralled her into depression and melancholia lasting years. It was at this uncle's memorial Theo became aware of Argyro.

At the house for the wake, when Argyro was serving guests coffee, Theo had inquired who her father was, and her answer pleased him, for her father had a respectable reputation. She had not thrown herself at him as some girls had done and he found her attractive and dignified. Theo considered asking for her hand, but discreet inquiries led to the discovery that her family was very poor, so she didn't have a dowry. In those days it was expected that a girl's family should have a dowry to help her marry and contribute something substantial to her marriage. Furthermore, since Theo had struggled to provide his own sisters with their dowries, he therefore thought it only reasonable to receive a dowry himself from his intended's family. Where they lived, in neighbouring villages in Kalamata, the dowry custom was as well-understood and appreciated as the olive oil and goat cheese they produced. It was his sense of a "fair go" that had dampened his marriage plans! Consequently, he had departed Greece without asking for her hand.

What was Argyro like? She was of average height and build, with shortish, wavy, dark brown hair and hazel eyes. Argyro had a strong personality and character and was hard-working, fiercely patriotic and always tried to support her siblings. Further, she happened to be nine years Theo's junior. Now in Australia, four years after he had met her, Theo wanted to ease his loneliness and to start a family of his own. But after all this time would Argyro be willing to leave all her loved ones, willing to leave all that was familiar and dear; to emigrate to the new and strange land of Australia in order to wed Theo whom she hardly knew? Theo procrastinated considering the difficulties. Eventually though he bit the bullet, and determined to ask Argyro to marry him!

In the cafe, not long after his arrival, Theo, second left, is enjoying his glass of beer and a lunch with other Greeks in Hamilton.

Argyro aged 17 & 20 years and her uncle, Captain Panos Katsareas

Chapter 3
The Marriage Proposal

Theo finally determined to write a letter to Argyro's father to propose marriage and hoped she would agree to come and settle in Australia. Not realising the Australian Government would give her free passage, he offered to pay for her journey: a one-way ticket to Australia by ship. Meanwhile Argyro had left her remote village in the Kalamata region, and had moved to the capital of Athens, where she shared a flat with her older brother, Nick, who was studying at university there. At that time Athens was a thriving city and she luxuriated in its bustle and vibe.

Since she wanted to be a seamstress, Argyro studied diligently, enjoying all the various aspects involved in sewing and pattern-making. To her delight she found she had a natural flair for it. Everything she was taught was a sinch for her, so she was habitually the best in her class.

Consequently, when Argyro was told about Theo's offer of marriage, she found it very arduous to make a decision, as she didn't have any desire to leave her country, knowing full-well she would miss her family. Besides, she felt youthful hope and promise in the future; life was exhilarating for her and she loved her role and the company of new friends. Farming responsibilities and her mundane village life seemed ions away. Therefore, time moved on and she dissembled and pushed thoughts of Theo aside, heedless of his particular agony. Argyro quite forgot that

Argyro (right) walking with fellow students

Athens in the early 1950s

procrastination is the thief of time! Meanwhile, back in Australia, after six months of waiting, Theo had still received no answer from Argyro! What was going on? In desperation he wrote to his cousin Ilias, who was also his best friend. He begged Ilias to talk with Argyro, and to urge her to decide once and for all if she was amenable to his proposal.

In order to fulfill his commission, faithful Ilias left for the city immediately. Of course he knew Argyro's whereabouts, because Argyro's brothers were his friends and everyone knows each other's business in a rural community. As he approached her shared abode, Argyro was chatting with her mother who happened to be staying with them for a few weeks. However, Argyro caught sight of Ilias through the window and she intuitively surmised why he had come: she remembered that Ilias and Theo were closer than brothers. Her idea proved correct because Ilias wasted no time telling her that lonely Theo was waiting with anxiety and in suspense for her reply.

Feeling embarrassed that she had been indecisive and indeed uncaring for so long, Argyro suddenly spoke what her heart had feared to decree, and told Ilias that she had already written to Theo the day before, accepting his offer of marriage! Ilias felt relieved that his undertaking had been so successful and he was certain Theo would be ecstatic! He did think it was serendipity: that her letter had been written just a day before he had visited! What providential good fortune for Theo!

In truth, Argyro wrote the letter to Theo the next day and posted it. Mail always took weeks anyway, so a day's difference would not signify in the least. Now that her decision was ultimately made there was no turning back! She would keep her word. After the Second World War, most Europeans were in poverty, and sadly for the women there were not many eligible young men. They were prized and could command an impressive dowry–something Argyro did not possess. To add to the difficulties of this issue, many unemployed men had left war-ravaged Europe to find work overseas, so men were at a premium, and Theo did not ask for a dowry.

As already mentioned, Argyro's family was poor, and her parents had nine offspring to care for. Argyro, being the second oldest, felt responsible to help them and it would be easier for everyone if she left for Australia to marry, even though she really deplored the idea of leaving her country. She was very patriotic and adored Greece, yet she was dismayed to be the one fated in her family to abandon it. Apprehension for her family constrained her to forsake her people and her country! Just as Theo had done before her, Argyro had based her decision to migrate, on her sense of duty, selfless love and concern for what was best for her family. Although she had seen Theo walking through her village and had heard other girls gossiping about him and hoping to meet him, she had only directly spoken to Theo several times. She recalled the memorial service of her maternal uncle, known as the *Eagle of Mani*, whom she had loved dearly and he had doted on her, carrying her on his shoulders when he was a teenager and she a little girl. She recalled poignant memories of his easy compliance with her tyrannical infantile demands, as she rode high and proud on his strong shoulders. Then, when she was seventeen, he had been shot and killed by the enemy. It had been an ambush on a lonely, rutted, mountain track while he was being driven in a jeep with three others. He had been only thirty-three years old. At her deceased uncle's three-year memorial service, Theo had first spoken to her. She knew she had made an impression on him, while serving coffee and dry cookies, dressed in black mourning clothes. Argyro felt her manner and her sombre eyes had touched his heart, for he had fought alongside her uncle. Clearly interested, he had asked her, "Whose daughter are you?" However, he had not proceeded with matters. Now years later she was going to Australia, considered a mysterious and wealthy land, to marry him: a comparative stranger. What a situation! Well, fortune favours the bold and she hoped to be lucky and happy with her decision to wed and emigrate. In those days Australia was truly at the ends of the earth, and nobody in Greece knew much about it.

However she had a reprieve: it took another one and a half years before she got her visa, since Theo had not known the requirements and procedures of sponsorship. After much effort and confusion dealing with bureaucracy, and with Andy's help, he finally posted her a ticket to Australia! Over the next few weeks, she cried till her eyes were swollen, instinctively knowing she would not see her loved ones for many, many years to come. (In fact, it would be twenty-one years before Argyro returned for her first visit.) Theo's younger brother, Panayiotis, made up one of the small number that had gathered to see her off at the harbour. He tried to cheer her up by making her think of her future. "I want to hear that you have had a son," he encouraged her. As the ship weighed anchor and gained distance from the ancient port of Pireaus, she wept to leave her life behind. Suddenly Argyro felt panicky: what was she doing leaving all that was familiar and loved? She climbed to the highest part on the stern of the ship, to catch a last view of her cherished land. Wanting her siblings to clearly distinguish her, she removed her rust-coloured coat and waved it like a flag, hoping they would respond. Argyro remained rigid until the land mass disappeared beyond the horizon. Then she slowly tread her way to her cabin.

In those days air travel was expensive and most emigrants travelled by ship and shared cabins as well. In the 50's, the Immigration Department of Australia, organised ships full of young women, who desired to come to Australia to marry the migrant men already employed as labourers. These ships were called "bride ships". Argyro boarded one such ship: the Tasmania. Ironically, it had originally been constructed to carry cattle, but now it carried eight hundred women, all going to Australia with the intention of marrying and starting families of their own! Since the Australian Government was planning to increase the population, it intended to settle the young migrant men in Australia. To this end, it offered free passage for these women, but Theo hadn't realised the case and had paid for Argyro's fare himself.

Argyro's first sighting of Australia was Fremantle, and some of the women were meeting their future husbands there. The ship was greeted by a flotilla of small boats crowded with men holding bouquets and calling out to the women. All the "brides" were permitted to disembark and walk on land for the first time in three weeks. They soon located the wharf's kiosk and gathered around the counter. Their only request was for a taste of fresh tap water! However, they couldn't speak English and the kiosk worker couldn't understand the Greek word for water, "νερό". Being of British descent, the kiosk worker had offered them cups of tea! The women felt exasperated because their simplest entreaty could not be grasped. Frustration was obvious as they experienced the language barrier for the first time. Mercifully, someone spoke the word "water" and the much anticipated, wonderful liquid tasted sweeter than honey, as it satiated their thirsts—but not their fears of things to come! How would they ever cope with English?

Leaving Fremantle after only a few hours, the *Tasmania* berthed in Melbourne five days later. The whole trip from Greece had taken twenty-eight days! What a welcome awaited the women on the ship! Hundreds of eager and excited young men were cheering and whistling, waiting on the wharf. Many carried bunches of flowers and there were streamers like cobwebs everywhere. At last, the hopes and dreams of hundreds of young men and women were about to collide with reality, as many faces searched for one another. Some women had never met their future husbands and recognised them only by looking at the black and white photos they held in their trembling hands. A number of women were disappointed by the actual men they apprised and returned to Greece unwed! Still others were pleasantly surprised. Argyro was luckier than some, because she had already met Theo, even though she had only spoken a few words to him and she didn't really know him at all, so she too feared for her future and ached for the familiar voices of family and friends.

Theo had sent Argyro a photo of himself as a keepsake, but she took exception to it, thinking he looked harsh. She didn't like to look at it. For this reason, during the trip, while her cabin mates had showed off photos to each other of their future spouses, she had not reciprocated. They had asked her, as girls do, "Is he handsome? Is he tall or short?" She had replied, "He is an old man." He was actually nine years her senior, but she was feeling self-pity. Consequently, they had left Argyro to her own devices, feeling sorry for her. They thought poor Argyro was going to marry an elderly man, and in her solitude, she continued to mourn the loss of her family and country.

Now, finally in Melbourne, looking down from the ship at the men, her cabin mates asked her. "Can you see him? Is he here?" Argyro pointed to a very tall, good-looking man in his early thirties. He was dressed in a suit and holding a bunch of red roses. "Oh, you were having us on! He really is a very handsome, young man!" they exclaimed, laughing and feeling relieved for her. "Good luck for your future. "Αντίο! Goodbye!" The date was January 4th, 1956.

Because the few Greek churches in Melbourne were inundated by couples seeking wedding ceremonies, Argyro and Theo were obliged to wait, and they married at the registry office. A day later they left with their official marriage certificate, for Hamilton. Months later, Theo invited a Greek Orthodox priest to come to Hamilton and marry them in a Church of England sanctuary, because there were no Greek churches in Hamilton.

Theo, with his typical generosity and in his eagerness to please his wife, had actually hired a taxi to drive the Greek priest all the way from Melbourne to Hamilton: a very expensive undertaking that cost a small fortune! So the morning following the wedding ceremony, Theo made a snap decision to put the priest on a plane for his return trip to Melbourne, a cheaper option. Andy Hadis who had a car, along with Theo and Argyro (still in their pyjamas) for company, quickly drove the priest to the Hamilton Aerodrome. Unfortunately, he missed his flight and they ended up with the priest insisting on driving the car himself all the way back to Melbourne. Then, still dressed in their pyjamas, they returned to Hamilton since they needed to open the cafe the next day!

Argyro is seen 2nd left in the back row, with her family soon after World War 2.

inside the Anglican Church, 22 Gray Street, Hamilton

They made a lovely couple on their wedding day. Argyro wore a beautiful bridal-gown they bought from Rockmans, a dress shop in Hamilton. It was covered in beautiful French lace.

Argyro's village, Saint Nikonas is in Mani, south of Sparti, on the mountains near the southern coastline. The people are known for their independence and ruggedness; it was from there the uprising started on 6/3/1821 against the 400-year-old Ottoman occupation. The World Factbook

Panayiotis with Argyro awaiting her departure for Australia

Chapter 4
Family

In March 1956 the Olympic Games came to Melbourne and the nation was excited about the famous track athlete, John Landy. He ran his famous preliminary race with the support of the entire country. However, at Olympic Park in Melbourne, when he stopped to help fellow runner Ron Clarke, who had tripped, he won the hearts of the world with his gallantry and sportsmanship! He became known as *Gentleman John*.

Argyro hadn't gone to the Olympics and struggled to settle in Hamilton, which, being a rural town, offered no English classes for her to attend and ease the process. Anyway, a migrant was expected to somehow learn English on their own, and to emulate the Aussie way of doing things. Also, there was little interest in other cultures, so new-comers were expected to assimilate and to change their "old" way of life. Furthermore, since Australians didn't understand "foreign" cultures, they were often intolerant of them. "Go back to where you came from!" was sometimes the comment made to migrants, or "Speak English like Australians!"

The British culture was prevalent and promoted through the education system, as Australians were Anglophiles and England was the "motherland". The *White Australia Policy* encouraged white, and especially British, immigrants to Australia. In fact from 1944 to 1949 a British subject living in Australia, automatically became an Australian citizen!

As it happened, Argyro fell pregnant soon after her marriage and went to hospital to have her first child. Of course it proved a stressful time for her because she didn't understand what the midwives were trying to communicate to her, so the entire experience was terrifying. She was also burdened with the shame of her ignorance of English. If only she could understand what the nurses were telling her to do! To make things worse, men were not allowed to be with their wives in the labour ward, so Theo waited in another room for news of his wife and baby. In his heart, he probably yearned for a son to carry on the family name, as it was a very important part of his culture. Theo wanted to name his future son "Peter" after his own father who had passed away when Theo was barely out of his teens. In this way he could honour his father's memory.

Argyro gave birth to a perfect, tiny infant who secretly, disappointed her mother, because *she* was not a *he*. All Argyro could think about were her brother-in-law's words, "I want to hear you have had a son!" She wished she had given her husband a son. After the delivery, Theo was taken to see his daughter in the nursery. He could not prevent feelings of disappointment, but being a pragmatist, he soon swallowed his negative thoughts. When he was allowed to see his wife, Argyro thought she detected something of disapproval in him. She started to weep and refused to take her newborn from the nurse, feeling very confused, homesick and disappointed: her hormones were playing havoc with her emotions!

However, the nurse assumed Argyro had not understood and soon thrust the small bundle of new life into her arms. Argyro's attitude changed as she nursed her daughter. Theo encouraged his wife by reassuring her that this was their precious child and they would love and cherish her. Theo did indeed love and cherish his daughter, naming her Voula, after his mother. Maybe the next child would be a son…

In fact, the next two babies were both sons, Peter and Demetrius (Jimmy), so Theo and Argyro were well satisfied that they had "done their duty" and the family name would continue for another generation. Later in life they would have a grandson named Theo, born to their first son, Peter. So the tradition of names continued unbroken.

Argyro taught her children the Greek language and culture. As Argyro still missed her family, it helped her to talk to her small offspring about her loved ones in her motherland. By this time, Theo had moved his young family into a rental house next to the local primary school. Hamilton had some beautiful houses and this one was a large, Victorian-style house with high ceilings and a big, solid-timber front door.

Everything was going well for the little family. However, the unexpected always happens and one day his little son, Peter, got his hand squashed as the heavy, front door closed on it. Argyro didn't know what to do to ease the pain, so she did what the old women in her village had done: she chopped up onions and garlic, added oil and vinegar, put it all on a tea-towel and then wrapped up the injured hand with the tea-towel for a bandage. It was a poultice to take away the bruising. Anyway, it got better!

Because of the primary school next door, there were a lot of interesting sounds coming from over the fence. It was a cacophony of yelling, cachinnating children at play. It was very intriguing for little Peter and Voula, so they sometimes stood on chairs to look over the fence at the primary school children playing in the school yard. It was opportunistic for the school children, who often teased them and were not very kind at all, because they regarded Peter and Voula as busybodies, sticking their noses over the fence! Also the little "wogs" didn't seem very friendly, because they *wouldn't* speak to the Aussie school kids for three reasons. Firstly, they were too shy; secondly, they couldn't speak much English and lastly they were aged two and three and didn't know much anyway!

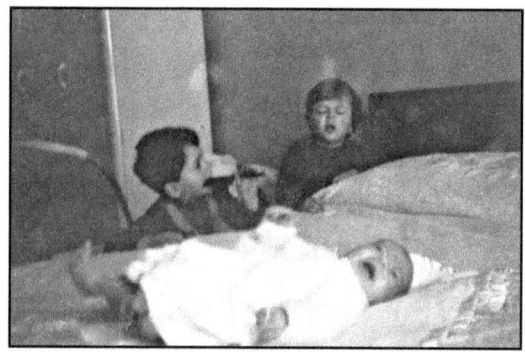

The family became complete in 1960 with the birth of "The Baby", Jimmy.

Argyro sewed lovely clothes for her children. They are standing in front of the "veggie patch" soon after moving to their own place in Byron Street.

Peter is standing in the front yard of the beautiful Victorian style house Theo rented.

a dilapidated old cottage that still stands on the fringes of Hamilton, perhaps dating back to the 1850s (2007)

Chapter 5
School

Finally, the day arrived when Voula reached the age of five and had to start preps. She found herself in a strange new world of blah, blah, blah and she was scared of school for a very long time! Voula learnt that she had to be silent and not speak until she was spoken to. That was not a problem since she could barely speak any English at all! Everything she learned was by copying what the other kids did. If they stood up behind their little chairs, so did Voula. If they walked to the front of the class and sat on little mats, so did she also. Everything seemed very strange. Her impressions of the teachers were that they were very tall and strict. Even the school uniform she wore did not protect her or hide her differences: she was still unlike the other kids because of her olive skin and she had no freckles like a lot of the sun-burnt Anglo-Saxon kids.

To make things worse, one day, Argyro decided to shave off all of Voula's hair with a razor: to make it "thicker" because she thought it was too fine. Argyro thought it was nice for girls to have lots of lovely, thick hair! Well! Voula had an even more difficult time at school, because at playtime the children pulled off her beanie to laugh at her bald, shiny head. All of this simply worked to ostracise Voula even more from her peers, as none of them wanted to associate with such a strange creature.

The children were taught to read from a "reader" called *John and Betty*. Voula took her turn going to the teacher's desk, to read

John and Betty out loud to her. She read one or two pages per day and when she got to the end she read it again until she felt confident and fluent. Then she received her next reader, which was more challenging.

The books were very focussed on the traditional bourgeois roles of girls and boys in Britain: boys played with trains and girls with tea-sets. After a year Voula was able to understand some basic English and when the children taunted her and said they could "boss her around," Voula retaliated with, "No, you can't!" Her response only made them tease her more by saying, "You don't even know what that means!" Voula had defended herself with the words, "Yes I do!" They had persisted, "Go on then: prove it!" So Voula took a girl by the hand and pulled her around and around herself, in a circle. That is what she understood by "boss around". Of course the children jeered even more and Voula felt estranged as the bullying continued. She felt alone, fearful and poles apart from the other kids. Most children like to feel they belong and are accepted by their peers. Nowadays schools have policies against bullying, but even so, it still persists in schools. It seems that children can be very cruel to one another.

Not many "wogs" resided in Hamilton in those days. Probably there are still not too many there today either. Life was tough for "New Australians" as they were not accepted by many Aussies. There were no pizzas, olives, Feta cheese, delicatessens or newspapers printed in other languages, except maybe in Melbourne itself. There were no McDonald's or Pizza Huts either. The Australian Government expected "New Australians" to magically become Aussies, by assimilating and not holding onto their own cultures. It was different then; many people were racists and there were no anti-discrimination laws and no English language schools. Consequently, when Peter and Voula started school they had a difficult time, because other children called them rude names and wouldn't let them join in with their games at play-time. Therefore, Theo and Argyro decided to send their younger son, Jimmy, to kindergarten to give him a head-start with the Aussie culture. Neither Voula nor Peter had gone to kindergarten, but it was a good idea, because by the time Jimmy started primary school, he had made many friends and was accepted by his play-mates. Also he could speak English very well.

Jimmy, Peter and Voula walked to the cafe every day during their lunchtime. It was only a block away, so it took them five or ten minutes to get there: depending on if they ran or dawdled. You can imagine the nice hot meals they enjoyed at Lucas Cafe. So, while their schoolmates ate Vegemite sandwiches the three siblings munched on steak, chips and salad. Sometimes they had time for ice-cream and jelly or fruit salad for dessert! The other children always wanted to know what they had eaten for lunch: they were a bit envious.

By the time Voula was in grade three, it was her job to take little Jimmy to kinder three days a week, during her lunch-break. You see, by then, Argyro couldn't take him there herself since she was working as a waitress in the very busy Lucas Cafe; lunch was their busiest time and they were flat out!

Voula would try to make her little brother, Jimmy, hurry his feet along, as she pulled him by the hand on their way to kindergarten, but the little fellow couldn't walk very fast and Voula was often late returning to school after lunch. Following lunch, the school often held assemblies to give out information to the adults and children, as printing of newsletters didn't happen in those days. For Voula, the most embarrassing times were when the whole school was outside, in the yard, having *Afternoon Assembly*. Unfortunately, when she was late, assembly had already started, and she was seen by all the teachers and kids as she ran through the gates, for about 75 metres, to join her class. It was her public shame; especially since it was drummed into the pupils that it was important to be punctual.

The head teacher, or Head Master, Mr. Harris was a short, plump, balding, kind-looking man, but he also knew how to be stern. Voula was scared of him and often felt her heart pounding and her face flush red as she ran into the school yard, after taking Jimmy to kindergarten.

Many times she was late, in front of everyone! She always felt mortified as she ran to her class group and joined them! If only the earth would open up and swallow her! Each time it happened she promised herself she would never, ever be late again, but sadly…without success! She never seemed able to keep to her convictions and felt powerless to improve her situation. The teachers' attitudes varied, because they were sometimes sympathetic of her situation and sometimes they scolded her for her tardiness!

Chapter 6
School Ceremonies and Rituals

For Hamilton's Gray Street State School, every Monday morning was *Assembly Day* for the entire school, except for the Infant Department which comprised of the preps, grades 1 and grades 2. It was thought the little ones did not have the stamina to cope with long speeches and ceremonies, so they held their own assemblies when they learnt nursery rhymes and songs together, sitting on little mats on the floor of the inside quadrangle.

Regardless of their *maturity*, Assembly seemed quite long to the older pupils too, as they collected in their grades and waited in a big U shape on the netball courts, in front of the school. On the left side of the school was a flagpole and every year a privileged sixth-grade boy had the honour of slowly raising the Australian flag while the school sang the National Anthem. In the 1960s, Australians sang the British National Anthem as their own, and Australia's population ranged between ten and eleven million: most of whom were Anglo-Celtics. (In 1947, the population was 90% British; in 1988 it was 74.55%; in 1999 it was 69.88% and in 2021 it had reduced to 39.8%.) On a following page are the lyrics and music of the first verse of the National Anthem, which was the only one the children learnt.

Singing the anthem was a very integral part of school life and it was also considered an honour and a duty to show respect to your country. Young and old stood whenever the National

Anthem was played at any public event. Voula certainly felt proud to be part of this ceremony. It was taken very seriously and the children had to show respect by standing upright with feet together and looking straight ahead at the flag. No speaking or fidgeting was tolerated and was punishable.

Furthermore, to ensure the pupils stayed in tune while singing, some of the school recorder band played the music. Just before the recorder band commenced, a drum roll was played by an envied drummer boy, who stood by the flagpole and thus introduced the anthem. Everyone was jealous of that boy because they thought he had the best job in the school,... except for the boy who raised the flag (that was probably the best job of all!). Immediately after the anthem, the boys saluted the flag and the girls curtsied, gently spreading their skirts.

An *Afternoon Assembly* was sometimes held after lunchtime. The children gathered in their grades again, on the netball court, to listen to relevant announcements and information that the teachers wanted to tell them. Furthermore, it was the time to praise and to honour high academic achievers, or children who had performed outstanding good deeds. When their names were announced, these children went out the front to stand beside the Head Master. He would say a few words about their achievements and thank them, shaking their hands and smiling. Then everyone admired them and clapped for them.

It was for these assemblies that Voula was often late attending, because she used to walk Jimmy to kindergarten during lunchtime. One summer day, poor Voula had managed to run all the way back to school from kindergarten, without being too late for Afternoon Assembly. As she stood under the hot sun, she started feeling dizzy, her knees started to feel wobbly and she heard ringing in her ears: that was the first time in her life that she fainted! Luckily she didn't hurt herself as she fell over onto the children near her before she hit the ground.

Anyhow, following the raising of the flag, the children placed their right hands on their hearts and recited the Patriotic Declaration: "I love God and my country. I honour the flag, I will serve the Queen, and cheerfully obey my parents, teachers and the law."

Not many schools have an oath like that anymore and even the "Oath of Allegiance" for new citizens has been replaced by the "Australian Citizenship Pledge". The pledge is taken by those becoming Australian Citizens during *Citizenship Ceremonies* when they promise to honour their new country and its laws. Here it is:

"From this time forward, (under God,) I pledge my loyalty to Australia and its people, whose democratic beliefs I share, whose rights and liberties I respect, and whose laws I will uphold and obey." The Government Immigration website explains that: "Repeating this pledge is the final step in becoming an Australian Citizen. By repeating the pledge, new citizens are making a formal and public commitment to Australia, including the responsibilities and privileges of citizenship." http://www.immi.gov.au

Back in the 60s, following the Patriotic Declaration, the Gray Street State School pupils sometimes sang their *school song*, which they needed to practise, so they could sing it at school athletics and swimming carnivals, where they competed against other schools. The school song served to bind the spirits of the pupils into one cohesive, proud body. It must have been successful, because the school had a proud history of accomplishments, with trophies and an honour roll of champions' names on the wall outside the Head's office. Here are some of the words of the school song:

"We girls and boys of Gray Street,
Hamilton 295,
We work and play together, …"
"In basketball and swimming,
We always do our best..."

The school had four *Sports Houses* named after native Australian birds: the Kookaburras, the Magpies, the Wrens and the Cockatoos. All the children of a family were kept in the same House to avoid family contentions. Voula, Peter and Jimmy were Kookaburras. Sometimes the School Houses would assemble at the four corners of the front grounds, each corner being occupied by a separate House. Then marching music would be played over the Public Address System, the PA, in 4/4 time and each child in each House stretched out their arms to align themselves to the child in front and beside them. They formed perfectly even columns and rows and then the House Captains called out, "Left, right, left, right, left, left …," until everyone helped each other to lift the same leg at the same time. They all marched on the spot with their arms swinging like pendulums and looking straight ahead until ordered to go. Each House group marched straight ahead to the next corner of the grounds and then had to turn the corner without losing their step and neat, orderly formations. It was an exercise in co-operation and united effort which was competitive as well.

It was very enjoyable to spend some time marching. The winners were those deemed "best marchers" by the judges: usually the senior teachers. Each house was awarded points which went towards the end-of-year tally and was part of the *House*

Sports scores. House Sports included an Athletics Carnival and a Swimming Carnival every year. Peter and Jimmy sometimes won their event, but Voula always came second or third in running because a tall girl, Julie, always beat her. Voula didn't know about training and did not discipline herself to practise, so she never actually came first, although she tried very hard on the day of the event. Maybe the butterflies in her tummy got the better of her!

Another important school ritual was the drinking of a free, half-pint of fresh, full-cream, dairy milk. Every day, just before morning playtime, the class *Milk Monitors* would go to a designated area and collect a crate of milk bottles for their grade. Back in class, they had the pleasure of using a pointy wooden stick to put holes in all the aluminium lids, and then to put straws through the holes. When the milk bottles were ready, the class walked past and each child took a bottle, went back to their seat, and happily drank up the creamy milk. Sometimes the crates of bottles were forgotten out in the sun for too long and they were a bit warm, but everyone still drank their milk. People did not know about lactose allergies back then, and no one was allowed out to play until they had drunk up all their milk!

Mr Harris,
Headmaster of State
School No. 295

Gray Street State School as it stands today, little altered from the 1960s, except for the position of the flagpoles.

The National Anthem

God save our gracious Queen! Long live our noble queen!

God save the Queen! Send her victorious, happy and glorious

Long to reign over us God save the Queen!

Chapter 7
Imperial Australia

It was April 17th, 1965, the day after Good Friday. Theo's and Argyro's three children were waiting for the bakery van to deliver their Hot Cross Buns. Argyro had put in her order two weeks earlier and now the day had arrived for the buns. The Kings Bakery, in Brown Street, is still there opposite Melville Oval in Hamilton. Also, many businesses are still owned by well-known local families. Back then in Australia, there were no fast food chains to go to whenever you felt like it, or late night shopping hours. When the shops closed at 5:30pm, you had to wait till the next day to buy what you wanted. Even nowadays, regular shopping hours in Hamilton mean shops close at 5:30pm Monday to Friday; at 12pm on Saturday and shops do not open at all on Sunday which is "the day of rest". Some stores have late trading hours. The first fast food store to open in Australia was *Kentucky Fried Chicken*, in Sydney in 1968. KFC was also the first fast food store to open in Hamilton, and everyone watched the advertising on TV: the chicken was "finger-licking-good".

On the Saturday that the children waited for the bakery van, the shops closed at noon, so they expected it to deliver their buns some time in the morning. Their noses were glued to the lounge window as they waited with anticipation to see it arrive. They loved the delicious buns as they were a special treat, because they only got *one* Hot Cross Bun every year, for Easter. Hot Cross Buns were as precious as gold! As the kids watched, they saw the van pull up in front of their house and they excitedly called their mother. Argyro went to the door to greet the delivery man and receive the paper bag of buns. Once the children received their buns they admired and smelled the fruity, cinnamon aroma.

How to make their bun last for as long as possible was their utmost thought. Voula had developed a technique which may be familiar to many children. It went like this: the white cross on top was gently peeled off for eating last; then the sultanas popping out the top, sides and bottom were pulled off and chewed individually to enjoy the sticky sweetness of their juices and lastly, the bread was peeled apart in thin layers and hung above the mouth in ribbons, before being savoured piece by piece. In schools around Australia children were taught to anticipate these buns as part of Easter, celebrating the resurrection of Jesus Christ following His crucifixion on the cross; hence the white cross on top of the buns. They were often served hot with butter spread on top. The commercial side of things with the Easter Bunny had not taken hold in society. Hot Cross Buns were sold in England in the nineteenth century. Generally they were sold by street vendors to the cry of "Hot Cross Buns".

While in primary school, Jimmy, Voula and Peter, along with thousands of other children across Australia, were taught to sing a particular English nursery rhyme. The lyrics go like this:

Hot Cross Buns! Hot Cross Buns!
One a penny two a penny – Hot Cross Buns
If you have no daughters, give them to your sons
One a penny two a penny – Hot Cross Buns!

As pennies, shillings and pounds were used in Australia when

Voula was in grade 3, in 1965, she was taught the values of the British imperial currency and weights by rote, along with the 12 times tables. However, on the 14th February, 1966, the "old currency" was withdrawn from circulation fairly quickly, and replaced by dollars and cents. Within as little as six months, it was quite unusual to see any shillings and pennies in circulation, although the odd coin still turned up here and there for years. So in 1967 all Australian pupils had to learn the new Metric System using dollars and cents, which of course is easier, being based on the ten times table.

Even though Australia gave up the Imperial System of measurement and currency, it was not prepared to give up the royal family! The Hamilton Botanical Gardens boasts a bust of Queen Elizabeth's grandfather King George V and in the 1960s, most classrooms in Gray Street State School had a photo of Her Majesty on the wall. Queen Elizabeth II ascended the throne on Feb 6th 1952, after the death of her father, King George VI. Everyone seemed fascinated with the new queen. Even Australia's then Prime Minister, Robert Menzies, admired and supported her because, during the royal tour of 1963, he praised Queen Elizabeth II by famously quoting a poem written by Thomas Ford, from the era of Queen Elizabeth I (1533-1603), "I did but see her passing by and yet I love her till I die". Everyone was a monarchist back then. The *Australian Women's Weekly* loved all things British and featured a royal guard outside Buckingham Palace on its front cover on 3rd June 1953. Most printed magazines were in drab black and white, with only the cover in colour, as it was very pricey. However, women's magazines couldn't resist using colour spreads inside the magazine, showing the queen's elegant and co-ordinated outfits.

The Australian's Women's Weekly commemorated her first visit to Australia in 1954, showing her smiling and happy with Prince Philip, on Sydney Harbour. Moreover, Hamilton was particularly honoured by a visit from the Queen and her husband, the Duke of Edinburgh, on February 26, 1954. One home, in Ballarat, even displayed a huge crown in their front yard to show their support for the monarchy, but all to no avail for the Queen's itinerary did not include Ballarat. Despite a lot of lobbying by regional towns, only Mt Gambier and Hamilton were chosen, so some of the other towns in the Western District felt bitterly disappointed!

Hamilton residents celebrated the queen's visit by decorating their windows with royal pictures, red, white and blue paper streamers and flags. When Her Majesty and the Duke arrived at the Hamilton Aerodrome at 4 o'clock, they were welcomed by around 1000 eager locals. Everyone was dressed to the nines, wearing hats, suits and gloves. The couple were met by the mayor and his wife and then driven down Gray and Lonsdale Streets to Melville Oval, where about 13,000 school children had been assembled since 8.00am. These children were from 175 different schools and were grouped behind rope barriers. They didn't wear hats for protection against the hot sun and some fainted in the heat and were taken to sick bay!

Fortunately, the Mother's Club had organised extra sandwiches, fruit, cool drinks and ice-creams for the children. Along with the children were several thousand other visitors, many of whom had travelled long distances for a glimpse of the royal couple. The Canberra Times reported 50,000 people present, which is a lot considering Hamilton's population was about 11,000! After being driven round the oval, between the lines of cheering and excited children, a little girl offered a bouquet to the Queen and then the couple were taken along Foster and Bree Streets to the aerodrome, for their flight to Melbourne.

When the queen returned to Australia for her second visit in 1963, she was again greeted by enthusiastic crowds. Argyro had collected a whole stack of *Australian Women's Weeklies*, because she loved the many colourful photos of the queen wearing gloves, hats and often holding a matching handbag.

As a point of interest, it was from this poem that Prime Minister Menzies quoted his respect and love of the Queen.

As already mentioned, the poem was penned by Thomas Ford (1580 – 1648) who was an English composer, lutenist, viol player and poet.

There is a lady sweet and kind,
Was never face so pleas'd my mind;
I did but see her passing by,
And yet I love her till I die.

Her gesture, motion, and her smiles,
Her wit, her voice, my heart beguiles,
Beguiles my heart, I know not why,
And yet I love her till I die.

Her free behaviour, winning looks,
Will make a lawyer burn his books;
I touch'd her not, alas! not I,
And yet I love her till I die.

Had I her fast betwixt mine arms,
Judge you that think such sports were harms,
Were't any harm? no, no, fie, fie,
For I will love her till I die.

Should I remain confined there
So long as Phoebus in his sphere,
I to request, she to deny,
Yet would I love her till I die.

Cupid is winged and doth range,
Her country so my love doth change:
But change she earth, or change she sky,
Yet will I love her till I die.

https://en.wikipedia.org/wiki/Thomas_Ford_

Her Majesty (circa 1950)

bust of King George V, Hamilton Botanical Gardens

the cover of The Australian Women's Weekly, February 1954

3 June 1953 Women's Weekly cover showing a royal guard

top: *a crown in a front yard* in Ballarat
(photo supplied by Helen Jenkin) below: *The Queen accompanied by Prime Minister, Mr Menzies, on March 10, 1954. He looks rather chuffed!*

above: Nurses on the balcony of Hamilton Hospital are greeting the Queen and waving flags.

_{Hamilton rocked in Royal salute (1954, February 27). The Argus (Melbourne, Vic. 1848 - 1956), p. 7. http://nla.gov.au/nla.news-article26593444}

below: Hamilton residents await the Queen's car. Most women are wearing hats, gloves and coats, while the men are dressed in hats, ties and suits. (photo supplied by Helen Jenkin)

The men have removed their hats as a mark of respect for the Queen as her car passes by.
(photo supplied by Helen Jenkin)

Theo is holding his godchild, Peter, and Argyro has Voula. (early 1957)

Chapter 8
ANZAC Day

It was April 25th, ANZAC Day, and Argyro and Theo were among the Hamilton residents as they prepared to watch the Diggers, wearing their ribbons and medals on their chests, march somberly along Gray St. As the soldiers marched in the parade, their children often marched proudly beside them. It is still an Australian institution and the marching still continues in Hamilton to this day. (Refer to the Internet for the ANZAC Day notice and the times of events.)

In the 1960s they assembled at the corner of Kennedy and Gray Streets at 9:45am. It was always the same every year. Then, at 10 am the marching would commence, led by a brass band in full regalia, along with some bag pipers and drummers too. It was a very reverential and colourful occasion. Also, it was a significant event and many people would turn out to pay their respects.

As people started to line the street outside Lucas Cafe, Theo, his partner Andy, and whatever children happened to be at the shop, would all come out and wait along the road to watch the parade. Peter, Voula, Jimmy and Andy Hadis' children felt excited and very respectful of the war veterans, because Argyro and Theo had told them the returned soldiers had fought for our freedom and way of life here in Australia and in Greece.

As the ANZAC Day marchers followed the Hamilton Brass band, they were greeted with applause from the onlookers lining

Gray Street. They then turned left and continued down Brown Street, before entering Melville Oval.

The procession then moved towards the Melville Oval cenotaph and the crowd was asked to clear the way for marchers as they entered the oval via the Royal Australian Air Force gates. Silence descended as voices were hushed and cars stopped or were diverted away from the intersection opposite the oval. The Hamilton Returned Services League sub-branch president always opened the ceremony with a speech. It may have been as follows:

"A time to be born, a time to die, ... a time for war and a time for peace."

Later, wreaths were laid at the foot of the cenotaph by many district organisations and schools. Then, after an emotional rendition of "Abide With Me," the crowd joined in "The National Anthem," and marchers then re-grouped and continued along Lonsdale St before being dismissed for another year.

At the oval were hundreds upon hundreds of little white crosses pegged into the grassy ground. Each one represented a fallen Digger from Hamilton and the surrounding area. The children were soon free to wander about and read the names on the crosses, as well as to inspect the wreaths at the memorial.

Another day of respect for soldiers, was *Remembrance Day*, otherwise known as *Armistice Day* or *Poppy Day*, which is still held every November on the 11th day. At 11 o'clock there was absolute silence in the school. It was introduced a couple of minutes before time, over the Public Address System, and everyone had to stop what they were doing and reflect on the soldiers who had given their lives for Australia's freedom. In Hamilton, even the cars on the streets stopped while drivers paid their respects to the courageous soldiers who would never return home to their grieving families.

On that day, in 1918, the Germans asked for an armistice, in order to obtain a peace settlement and their final surrender to the Allied Forces. Later, fake poppies were sold and the proceeds given to war widows and their families. Red poppies were among the first to flower in the terrible battlefields of Belgium and northern France during the First World War. Worn on lapels on Remembrance Day, each year, they commemorate the ultimate sacrifice as, according to the soldiers, the bright red colour of the poppy was due to the blood of their fallen comrades soaking into the ground. Second World War veterans are so few and fragile nowadays, that they are usually driven in cars, so they can still be part of the ANZAC Day Parade. Of course ANZAC Day is a public holiday and many people enjoy the break from work and the opportunity to support the war veterans.

Diggers marching in 1953

Voula, 6 years old, is kneeling beside Peter and Jimmy in front of the cenotaph. Her hair had grown back after being shaved off by Argyro. The Hadis boys are on her right. Notice the white crosses pinned into the grass, in the background.

Today, Hamilton's Monivae College Band participates in the Anzac Day march. (used by permission of Monivae, Feb. 2016)

Chapter 9
Katie and The Beatles

Voula was very excited but tried to contain herself. According to her mother, a teenage *Australian* girl was expected any minute for a visit! Apparently, an acquaintance of Argyro, had a 14-year-old daughter, Katie, who was just mad about The Beatles pop group. The problem was that Katie didn't have a TV and wanted to watch them on the live broadcast from Melbourne. "My pleasure," Argyro had replied, "Katie can visit and watch on our new Healing TV." (It also had a radio with push-buttons and above that a record player. It was a state-of-the-art, 3-in-1 unit and it was the family's latest and grandest acquisition of a few months earlier. It had cost them a small fortune!)

This visit by Katie was rather intimidating because, up till now, Argyro had only ever invited Greek guests in her home, as she felt Anglo-Saxons would look down on her due to her poor communication skills. Also she never gave permission for her children to go on school camps or on sleepovers. Argyro felt her children might be disdained by the other kids, or that they may learn to belittle their Greek culture due to peer pressure and the influences of the pervasive British culture.

Today Argyro asked her daughter to make Katie feel welcome, but what could Voula do? She didn't have any experience! After considering her options, Voula went to the mirror and practised her smiling. She looked at her open smile showing her teeth and at her closed mouth smile. Which was better?

On Wednesday July 1st 1964, Katie knocked on the door to be greeted by a shy, but secretly elated Voula. What a great honour to have a *grown-up Australian* girl in her home! Katie settled on a sofa in front of the TV and Voula turned it on for her. "How do you change the channel?" enquired Katie. She asked this because she wanted to check the channels, uncertain as to where The Beatles would actually be showing. Katie thought it was HSV Channel 7, so Voula turned the dial to 7 and they sat there watching the screen and waiting for the show to start.

After a quarter of an hour had elapsed and there was still no appearance of The Beatles, Katie freaked! She forgot her polite manners and sat on the floor in front of the television, clicking through the channels. Finally she found the band playing on Channel 9 and was distressed that she had not caught the very start of the show. Katie's eyes were glued to the telly, so Voula's feeble efforts to chat and make Katie feel welcome and at home fell on deaf ears. To tell you the truth, seven and a half-year-old Voula wasn't interested in The Beatles; she was surreptitiously watching Katie.

Consequently, after a few minutes Voula noticed something very sad: Katie was crying! She sympathetically told Katie not to be sad and the horrible weight in her belly confirmed her fear that she had failed in her attempts at being a good hostess. Katie ignored her and Voula slowly began to edge away from her until she was sitting on the sofa, away from Katie. What should she do now? After a few more uncomfortable minutes of silence, Voula got up and walked into the kitchen to find her mother. "Katie doesn't want to talk to me. I don't know what to say and I don't want to be with her anymore." Argyro compelled Voula, "You must stay with her. It's rude to leave her alone and *I* don't know how to speak with her." Argyro's English had not progressed as far as that of her kids and she sometimes asked Voula to read business letters and interpret them to her. Her child hated doing it as it required more patience and comprehension than she possessed.

Now Voula did her best. She stood at the door of the lounge room and stared at Katie who was smiling and crying at the same time! "Why are you crying Katie?" she quietly asked. Katie made a perfunctory attempt to converse a little with Voula, "Because I love The Beatles so much. I just love them! I wish I was one of the people in the audience. My favourite Beatle is Ringo Starr. Who is yours?" Unfortunately, Voula did not even know The Beatles names. She didn't know that their song "Love Me Do" released in December 1962, had rocketed to the top of the music world. Not only that, but The Beatles had begun a phenomenon involving young men across the world: a new hairstyle craze, the "mop-top".

Voula stammered hesitantly, "I like them all the same. They're all pretty good." Katie looked at Voula suspiciously, correctly surmising the child before was an ignoramus! (It is well known that if you ask no questions you'll hear no lies.) After that Katie didn't speak to Voula and concentrated on admiring her idols and bopping to their music. She was determined to have a great time and that did not include making small talk with a little seven-year-old girl: The Beatles show would be over all too soon!

When the programme ended, Katie turned off the television, much to Voula's surprise as she had expected Katie would ask her to turn it off, out of politeness. Then Katie headed into the kitchen to thank Argyro. After that she made a quick exit and was never seen or heard of again. The whole experience left a strange impression on Voula and she decided that teenagers were very odd. She wondered if she would become like that when she was a teenager! Anyway it seemed an eternity away.

In fact about 45,000 people saw The Beatles six performances, and the last show was taped for television by Channel 9 and broadcast in Australia on 1st July from 7:30 to 8:30pm. The impact and popularity of the Beatles was not isolated to a few fans like Katie.

Several days later, at a reception inside the Melbourne Town Hall, the "cream of Melbourne society" gathered to officially welcome The Beatles to the City. The Sun reporter, Keith Dunstan wrote:

"At first, there was a hush and respectful clapping. Suddenly it was on. All around, girls were screaming, pushing forward, trying to stroke their jackets. Young ladies who five minutes before had looked very correct were screaming: 'WE LOVE YOU BEATLES'."

www.onlymelbourne.com.au/the beatles-melbourne

The revolutionary *youth culture* was about to explode onto the world stage and Australians bore witness to its birth!

the 3-in-one, state-of-the-art entertainment unit

The Beatles from left: George, John, Ringo and Paul

In 1964 Voula was in grade 2B comprising 40 pupils! She is in the second row behind the girl holding the blackboard.

Chapter 10
Music

Trams, traffic lights and so many cars on the roads! The country kids looked up out of the bus window at the tram wires criss-crossing the space above the Melbourne road. How was it possible to construct so many power lines for all the trams? Hamilton had no traffic lights or a single tram, no wide roads and no large shops. Voula wished that it did as it would add to Hamilton's consequence and significance. She continued to look in admiration and wonder as the bus travelled towards the Prahran hall where her school recorder-band was competing in the yearly eisteddfod against other Victorian schools. Gray Street State School usually did quite well in the musical competition.

It had all started for Voula in 1965 when she was in grade 3 and the music teacher, Mr Sullivan, had taught every child from grades 3 to 6 to play the descant (soprano) recorder. Argyro paid for Voula to have her own recorder which was made of wood and was a lovely light walnut colour. Children were invited to join the school Recorder Band if they wanted to commit to twice weekly lunchtime practices. By the time Voula was in grade 5, Mr Sullivan had asked her to play the treble, which was a larger recorder with different fingering. This recorder was of beautiful rosewood.

To aid the children to learn new pieces of music, Mr Sullivan wrote the music on large butcher's paper and helped them read the music by writing the letters above the notes. In this way he had taught the school Recorder Band various songs, using specific colours for the musical notation of the various musical instruments. He was a young, talented and enthusiastic musician and managed to harmonise the sounds of the various musical wind instruments, like the different recorders: tenors, trebles, descants and piccolos, as well as the melodicas. There were also several percussion instruments like glockenspiels, drums, triangles, cymbals, maracas and even a horn that was squeezed as the final note when a boy walked onto the stage, as a surprise finale.

That year the school band won a prize at the eisteddfod in Prahran and cut a small 7 inch record which participants purchased as a memento of the recorder band's success. They felt very proud of their school band. Childishly, they dreamed they would become famous, like The Beatles one day!

Each year when the band took the four and a half-hour drive to Melbourne, (because there were several stops too, for toilet breaks) the kids, teachers and some helper parents were first taken to a local primary school in Prahran. Here they were officially welcomed by the headmaster and pupils and given some refreshments. After that, their names were called out and they were introduced to the local children and parents, in whose homes they were to be billeted for two days. To try and avoid homesickness two or three Gray Street girls or two or three boys, were allocated to a volunteer family whose children were of similar ages.

The time spent at family homes was limited as they were taken to school with their new friends, after breakfast. During school times the Recorder Band were kept busy with activities and practising their music for the eisteddfod. Once the school day was over, the parents took all the children home for tea, supper and bed.

During the eisteddfod itself, the children had to wait their turn to perform. Speaking during a performance was forbidden and they learned to clap at the appropriate times, even if applauding a competitor or a terrible performance! Good behaviour meant being polite and doing the "right thing". Often it took hours before their school name was announced, so each year they entered the competition, they knew boredom was part of the experience. Young kids don't have much patience or stamina and Voula was no exception, although she did her best to be entertained and to enjoy the experience!

The following year it was the turn of Gray Street State School to host the children who had billeted the Recorder Band members. Voula shared her bedroom with two little girls from Melbourne. They were very shy and it was awkward for Voula to know how to spend time with them until it was bedtime. She took them for walks to show them her neighbourhood, showed them her stamp collection and shared her Spirograph drawing game. It was a bit of a relief when they departed after two days, because Voula was also shy and lacked confidence. At the end of 1968, Mr Sullivan announced he was leaving Hamilton and sadly the Recorder Band was disbanded. It had been a wonderfully rewarding experience for Voula and she kept playing her recorders.

Besides the Recorder Band, the school had a choir composed of grade 3 to 6 pupils. When pupils started grade 3, the choir teacher, Mrs. Criton, sought choir members and asked children to come and stand by her piano one at a time. Once there, she tested their pitch by playing a note on the piano and asking them to sing it, to determine if they were tone deaf. Voula was able to sing the right note and was invited to join up, so she did. When Peter was invited to try-out the following year, he refused saying the choir was for "sissies": singing wasn't his forte!

In 1968, the choir travelled by bus to Ballarat, a two and a half hour-long trip from Hamilton. The purpose was to appear on the local television station BTV Channel 6. This TV station held an annual Talent Quest and the choir had been invited to perform on television after gaining third place in the Ballarat Royal South Street Society, in the School Choral Contest, on 12 September 1968. The Royal South Street Society is still running musical and singing competitions, as well as dancing and debating ones.

The TV performance was not part of any competition but just for entertainment. Voula was in grade 6 and felt excitement mounting as the kids were arranged in rows on tiered timber planks and waited under the hot television lights. There were two cameras that rolled on wheels and behind each was a man who controlled it. When the camera was televising, the red light on top of it glowed. The singers started perspiring with the heat, but were told to look casual and unaffected as the camera scrolled across their faces. All the same Voula couldn't help feeling very self-conscious. However, things got worse when she got home.

It happened that one day, soon after her experience at BTV 6, Voula was walking home along Byron Street, when one of the "big boys" who lived on the corner, at the bottom of Billy-Goat Hill, approached swaggeringly towards her. She had always been intimidated by the four teenage boys who had formed a band with drums and electric guitars. They seemed "wild" and out of their parents' control. In fact only two of the four were brothers, while the others were constant visitors: maybe *they* dreamt of following in The Beatles footsteps. It's interesting how one's views are coloured by what is seen, although not knowing all the facts and Argyro had warned Voula to keep away from them, but now one of them strutted towards her, on his way home. To her amazement, as they got closer, he broke into a big smile. Voula automatically smiled back. Then he unexpectedly scowled threateningly and she lost her smile, her face changing uncontrollably. He grinned again and she smiled again. This was bizarre! She willed herself not to be a puppet in his control! Next time he smiled she kept her face neutral. As they crossed paths he said sarcastically, "Now we have a TV star in the neighbourhood!" Voula was surprised and didn't know how to respond for trepidation. Although she felt scared, she kept walking, refusing to run away. Her heart was pounding! She felt relieved he hadn't followed her. She held her breath as there was still time for him to change his mind and taunt her further. As the distance between them increased, she began to feel safer: apparently he was satisfied with his few words, and had said his bit! After that, whenever she was obliged to go down Billy-Goat Hill and pass his place, Voula walked on the opposite side of the road, and even checked to see if anyone was sneakily following her. It seems that fame may bring fleeting glory, but it brings problems too!

Argyro had asked Voula a question when she was nine years old, "Do you want to learn ballet or would you prefer piano lessons?" Voula had a romantic streak and loved the look of ballerinas in their elegant dresses and tutus as they gracefully pirouetted and spun on their tiptoes. Her bedroom curtains had lovely prints of ballerinas. So, after a few days of contemplating,

Argyro was very surprised to hear her daughter's decision, "Piano!" Practical little Voula reasoned she would probably outgrow ballet, but an ability to play piano would most likely be useful all her life. Argyro spoke with Theo and shared their idea with his business partner, Andy, asking for his counsel. They soon discovered there was an experienced music teacher, Mrs Hughs, a widow right across the road from the primary school, in Kennedy Street. It was decided that, to begin with, both Peggy, Andy's daughter, and Voula would share a music lesson. This would enable the parents to test the continued commitment of their daughters and save some money at the same time.

When the girls arrived at the house, Mrs Hughs set one of them to work on music theory, whilst she gave the other girl a 15 minute practical lesson; then they swapped. Mrs Hughs had very proper British ideas of behaviour, and as the girls were not her guests but paying students, they were not allowed to ring the front door-bell, but were instructed to use the "trades" entrance on the right side of the house. Once admitted, they noticed they were in a large dim room with several pianos. Some furniture was covered with sheets or blankets and there was antique furniture everywhere. The music teacher apparently earned money by French Polishing, and sometimes the room smelled of oil and alcohol when she answered her door.

Mrs Hughs was a senior lady but that didn't stop her from getting on the roof and fixing roof tiles. She must have been very fit! To her pupils, she appeared austere and distinguished, like a grand old lady, so they were always on their best behaviour.

Once, Mrs. Hughs confided in Voula, telling her that her husband had been a mayor of Hamilton, that she had been the first woman to graduate as an engineer from Melbourne

University, and that she was in the process of writing a book of her family history, entitled "Sleepers Two by Two". A couple of times Mrs Hughs asked that the girls extend their lessons as their abilities grew, although the system of sharing lessons continued for nearly three years.

Regrettably, the girls were too lazy and not self-disciplined, so they didn't practise much from one week to the next, even though Theo had taken his daughter to a music store, to chose an upright piano for her bedroom. He obviously encouraged Voula to do well in her musical skills, while in her turn Argyro tried nagging her to practise. Regardless, Voula's progress was minimal! After each dismal lesson, when it was clear she hadn't done her homework to practise her playing, Voula felt guilty and promised to practise, but she lacked the will power to fulfill it! Both Peggy and Voula completed their AMEB music exams to grade 3 level, mainly due to the tenacious and gracious Mrs Hughs, before the lessons came to an abrupt halt.

The "trades" entrance on the right was used by the girls as they were not "guests".

Spirograph patterns

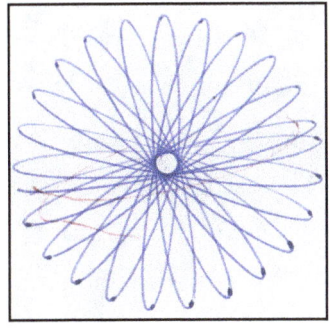

A sign of the times! Argyro dressed Voula like a young lady. Here, she is eight and a half years old and it is 29th June 1965.

Chapter 11
The Accident

It was the September holidays! In 1964, there were only three long, tedious school terms, not four like nowadays; so both teachers and children really looked forward to the holidays! Voula was nearly eight years old, while her brother Peter was six and a half and Jimmy was almost four.

Whenever Argyro helped out in the cafe, during the busy lunchtime hours, the three siblings spent their afternoons at Lucas Cafe, in the "Private Room," between the kitchen and the customers' dining area, playing board games and trying not to succumb to ennui. This involved reading the cartoon strips, or colouring-in the cartoon pictures in the old black and white newspapers stacked in the room for the purpose of wrapping take-away fish and chips. The newsagency next-door to Lucas Cafe, supplied lots of out-of-date newspapers. Moreover, every Thursday, new children's comic books were delivered next-door, so Jimmy, Peter and Voula looked forward to Thursdays for this reason, as their parents provided them with money to buy one each. Voula always took her time browsing the newly arrived comic books; smelling the new pages and deciding which to buy. It was a big decision. They usually bought "Jack and Jill", "Superman," "Super Heroes," or "Richie Rich" comics and then returned to the Private Room to spend as engrossing hour reading their comics and then swapping them for further interest.

Today was just a typical day in the Private Room and they soon grew bored. Jimmy didn't want to colour-in any more pictures in the comic strips; all the kids had a bit of cabin fever. Maybe they could go to Coles to get *Dairy Queen* ice-cream cones? Since it was a beautiful spring day, Argyro gave her children permission to go to Woolworths and look for little toys to buy. This was because Woolworths was closer than Coles, being only four shops away, down Gray Street. The kids would not be crossing any streets. If they turned right from the back gate of Lucas Cafe, into the laneway, Woolworths was on the corner, the first shop around from the lane. Woolies was more of a variety store in those days and it didn't sell much food. Customers looked at the goods on display along counters and asked a shop attendant serving behind the counters for help. Customers paid her and she put their items in a paper bag–no plastic bags were used then.

Argyro had told her kids that they had to go out the back of the shop through the lane, so they wouldn't get underfoot. Andy had told Theo it was bad for business, and looked unprofessional for patrons to see a bunch of snotty-nosed children hanging around inside the shop. Therefore, the kids avoided the crowded shop of lunch-time customers, by leaving through the back door, with strict instructions to hold Jimmy's hands and to take care of him. The kids had a threepence coin with them, in Peter's pocket, with which they intended to buy a small, plastic car or some marbles, for the boys. The older children obeyed the instructions to take Jimmy by the hands, as a precaution: Voula took him by one hand and Peter took his other one. Thus arranged, the three of them walked out the back door, passed the old dunny, passed the wood stack, through the gate and entered the quiet lane that was used by all the shop owners, to park their cars or to get delivery of goods for their shops. At the end of the lane they turned right into Thompson Street and continued walking along the red brick side wall of Woolworths. They had only taken a few steps when they heard a cheeky, shrill voice calling, "Jimmy come and play with me!" It was Jimmy's kinder friend, Chris, a little Greek boy and a family friend. His family owned a cafe near where he was standing, laughing and beckoning from across busy Thompson Street. Voula was about to open her mouth, to forbid Jimmy, when she felt his hand unexpectedly tug out of her grasp. "Why didn't I hold him more tightly?" she chided herself.

Then everything happened so fast that it felt surreal. The traffic stopped. Voula saw people running onto Thompson Street. As if in a dreadful nightmare, she suddenly realised with horror that Jimmy had been run over by a white ute! She saw that the driver had got out and was bending over Jimmy's small body under his vehicle! Voula turned away. She wanted to disbelieve the accident had happened! Maybe if she didn't look she could pretend it had not happened and that Jimmy would be unhurt. He *had* to be okay!

The distraught driver carried Jimmy to the footpath and lay him down where a lady knelt and took his head on her lap. Maybe...Jimmy wasn't hurt very much. Voula didn't want to look at her unconscious little brother, so she turned away and looked at the "bad" man who had run over her brother. He appeared to be a farmer wearing an Akubra hat and a thick jacket. At that moment Voula thought of him as her mortal enemy because of what he had done. He was looking down at the lady on the footpath and at the small boy whose head and chest wounds caused bleeding over her dress. Voula thought everything was wrong. Their mother should be here taking care of Jimmy and not this kind lady!

The woman looked distressed and was asking the gathering pedestrians if anyone knew of the boy's parents. Suddenly Voula wanted to acknowledge her brother, to help him. She found her quivering voice. "He's my brother," Voula heard herself inform the lady. The woman looked up at her and asked, "Where are your parents?" Then Voula understood she had an important role to perform. "I'll get them," she told the lady and turned, running past distraught Peter into the laneway.

With all her being Voula understood the urgency to return to the cafe, to her parents, to get help. However something was very baffling: her legs wouldn't obey her! They felt leaden and she found it difficult to move them at her will! It felt to her that her legs were trying to run in water. She was a sleepwalker in a nightmare! For a moment she believed the world had become insane, but she couldn't deceive herself for long. Voula thought it might be more productive to walk rather than try to run, but it felt too slow. Voula sobbed with frustration at her ridiculous ineptitude. She tried running again as her thoughts raced ahead to the problem of telling her parents about Jimmy, and of the pain they would feel at the news. Why did fate determine she would be the one to tell them such horrendous news? With a shock she realised she was *still* in the lane. It seemed time had slowed because it was taking ages to reach the back door of the cafe! Why couldn't she move faster just now, when she really needed to? It was extremely vital to be quick but she could not move fast enough!

Continuing her struggle to force her strange legs to obey her bidding, Voula finally reached the back door of the shop. It had taken an eternity! At last, she knew help was at hand: adults would take over the situation now! She could give her burden to a grown-up, who would know what to do. She felt inadequate and guilty for not looking after her brother properly. Would Jimmy be alright? How badly hurt was he? Would her parents blame her? Was he *still alive*?

Voula ran into the kitchen where her Uncle George was grilling steaks for lunches. "Jimmy's been run over!" she blurted out to him. Unbelievably, he laughed at her! Voula stared at him. She had not anticipated that he would not believe her. He thought she was pulling his leg! How could he possibly think she was teasing about something like this?! Her face screwed up in fear and consternation and she wrung her hands in her vexation. She started to moan as she tried again to persuade her uncle.

All of a sudden Voula heard hurried heels on the concrete floor and swung around to come face-to-face with her mother, who had just come into the kitchen with some dirty plates for the sink. There was an appeal and urgency in her voice as she cried out, "Mum, Jimmy's been run over!"

This time the reaction was completely different as the plates crashed and broke forgotten on the floor. "Yes, yes, it's true mum," Voula repeated fearing that her mama might doubt her after all. "Where is he?" demanded Argyro. Voula did her best to explain where she had left Jimmy.

Argyro ran through the shop to get Theo and together they left to locate their younger son. The whole shop was buzzing with the news, as the customers realised something was wrong and some of them ran out to see if they could help. Andy used the shop phone to ring for an ambulance.

Some time later, Voula realised Peter had joined her and

together they waited in the Private Room, throughout the afternoon. With the taste of fear in their mouths, they argued about the terror they found themselves in, and blamed each other for not holding onto Jimmy's hands tightly enough. Neither of them wanted the blame for the accident and we all know that attack is the best form of defence. They were scared stiff–witless with fear!

They waited hours for their parents to return, yet feared more what would happen next. It seemed so bizarre and strange that the world continued on, as if nothing had happened to destroy their peace!

The siblings are outside the newsagency and Jimmy and Peter are holding new comic book.

The children are at the Hamilton Baths during their September holidays before the accident.

Lucas Cafe, looking from the back "private room" of the shop towards the front door

Chapter 12
Celebrations

Two nights later when the children were in bed for the night, Voula heard her mum's footsteps as she entered her daughter's bedroom. "Are you asleep?" Voula heard her mother's voice and felt the movement on her mattress when her mum sat down beside her. Voula knew her mother had just returned from the hospital. "Will Jimmy be alright?" she enquired, yet fearing the answer. Her mother spoke with sadness, "Jimmy has lost a lot of blood. Also the doctors have grafted some of the skin from his thigh onto his chest. His left leg is broken and some ribs too. The doctors are waiting to see what will happen over the next couple of days. Please pray for him Voula, because I know God loves little children very much. Maybe He will hear your prayers and help Jimmy recover." Argyro and her little daughter wept together. Voula felt a lump in her throat–it was the pain of grief.

She was immensely relieved that her parents didn't blame her, or Peter, for Jimmy's accident. Their parents were not angry, but Argyro looked unspeakably sad and extremely weary, not having slept much at all. It was obvious that the doctors could do no more for Jimmy; now only God could succour him. "Jimmy is fighting for his life," thought Voula. That was the first time she seriously and consciously prayed to God; it was personal. "My brother, my little brother....please, please, please God save him!" She wept as she prayed and her tears felt hot as they ran down

Jimmy with his leg in plaster, is standing at the back door of the house.

her cheeks. The young girl felt like her world had collapsed and that life would never be the same again! Would God really save Jimmy? Voula prayed again, and as often as she remembered. She made a childish deal with God, that if He saved Jimmy she would believe in Him.

The loving hand of Providence did indeed intervene and Jimmy gradually recovered and was sent home with plaster on his leg. Theo carried Jimmy into the house and Voula knew God had given her little brother another chance at life! She was overwhelmed that God had heard her prayers. Her heart offered a paean of thankful joy at the realisation that God was *good* and *real*. Young Voula knew she could trust God and was overwhelmed with a sense of discovery! However, with time, and being spiritually unnurtured, the child soon misplaced God, growing uncertain in a disbelieving world, and having to struggle and search for the truth, the presence of God, in her future life.

Anyway, the family was overjoyed to have Jimmy back again and Argyro tended to his every whim. He was her special child because she had nearly lost him. Nothing was too much for Jimmy! Amazingly soon, life was back to normal again, except that Jimmy couldn't move very fast, or very far, for a few more months. In October, when Jimmy's fourth birthday got close, Theo rang the Hamilton newspaper, *The Spectator*. They agreed to send a reporter to come and write a story about the little boy who had survived the appalling accident of several weeks ago. They would also send along a photographer to take a photo for the article. Counting down the days until the birthday party, the family became very excited.

On the day of the party some of the neighbourhood kids and friends were invited. They all wore party hats, blew up balloons, ate lots of food and had too many lollies. Since Voula's birthday was only nine days after Jimmy's, the party was held for both of them together. Voula wore a hat with stars on it for the newspaper photo, which was put on the front page. It shows Jimmy in a bow tie and wearing a vest and shorts, but best of all are the smiles on Theo's and Argyro's faces. Their son was alive and well!! Understandably, their smiles were heartfelt, for they were very happy indeed and on top of the world!

School continued. The siblings and their classmates played games together. The girls liked: Hidey, Kick the Tin, Skippy, Elastic and Hop Scotch. The boys preferred playing footy and cricket or fighting games. The children were segregated because the boys played on the oval and the girls played their games on the tarred area.

When it rained everyone ran into the Shelter Sheds to wait for the bell to ring, so they could return to their classrooms. There, they could use the full-length seats along the walls to play the game of *Cat and Mouse*. The "Cat" stood in the middle of the shed and tried to catch the mice as they ran along the seats from their safe corner to another corner. When a "Mouse" was caught as it tried to run to a corner, it became the "Cat"!

Every year the school held a fancy dress parade. The children got dressed up as special characters and met outside the town's library. There, the teachers tried to arrange everyone in some sort of order for walking in the parade as people, mainly parents, waited in anticipation along Gray Street to applaud the parade. When the time came to begin, a brass band headed the parade as it walked down the street. The children followed the band and the parents, cheering and clapping, followed the children until everyone walked through the main gates onto the school grounds.

There the annual school fete was held and to commence, the headmaster thanked everyone and announced the winner of the dress parade. It was a bit of an honour to win! Voula won it the first year she wore her Greek National Costume when she was in grade 4. Her mother had spent long hours sewing it. The jacket was of deep red velvet and the skirt was of green silk. After that, she wore the same costume again and again, even when it became too small for her in grade six. Voula had asked her mum to make something else for her, but Argyro insisted that her children wear their National Costumes and show people they were proud of their heritage. Both Jimmy and Peter also wore their home-made Greek National Costumes in the school parade, year after year. However, Voula never won a prize for her costume again as people got used to seeing it every year.

At the school fete, pony rides were always a favourite. There too were mothers selling home-made cakes, biscuits and jams. There was a Merry-Go-Round and Fairy Floss. Also there were competitions to guess how many buttons or beans were in glass jar or to see who could throw a tennis ball the farthest.

A popular competition was the floral saucer competition judged by the Mothers Club. Children were invited to bring along a saucer of wet soil or sand and some flowers. They were allowed some time during school to arrange the flowers on their little mounds and position them in the library on erected tables. Many beautiful arrangements were on view there, with ribbons displayed for the ones that had won first, second and third prizes. Don't ask me how they were judged, for they were all beautiful!

During the fete, all the classrooms were open, so parents could walk in and admire their children's pictures on the walls and look into their neatened desks. It was a good family time and an opportunity for the school to raise funds to buy more equipment for the kids to use.

Every year Gray Street Primary School, Hamilton 295, had another tradition. At the end of the year, on the last day, the whole school walked in their grades to the Prince Regent cinema, two blocks away. The children walked in pairs chatting and holding hands as they made their way down Gray Street, passed Lucas Cafe and turned right at the end of the block. When all the school was seated inside, Mr Harris, the headmaster, stood on the stage to welcome them and wish everyone a happy holiday over Christmas. Then everyone stood up to sing the National Anthem, *God Save the Queen*, after which the lights went out and the movie would begin.

It was a lot of fun and very exhilarating to watch a movie together as a school. Usually, the first film was a comedy. At half time, after the first movie, the teachers gave each pupil an ice-cream to enjoy too. After the interval, the second movie or feature length cartoon would begin. Of course, in those days there was no sex or violence in movies. The worst thing you could see was *Cowboys* shooting *Indians* or having a gunfight, but there was never any blood!

Disneyland movies were very popular and the school saw many Disney films over the years. *Bambi, Snow White and the Seven Dwarves and Story of Cinderella* were some of them. After the movies, the children were pleasantly tired and ready to return to school for their class cleanups and goodbyes. Often the kids were sent to visit their new teacher and to sit in the classroom they would graduate to the following year. The change was as good as a holiday and was all part of the thrill of the last day of school, before it was time for home and the summer holidays!

In their National Greek Costumes walking in the parade, Jimmy looks self-conscious while Voula has outgrown hers.

Peter G, dressed in his cowboy costume, awaits the start of the parade.

the newspaper photo that appeared in The Spectator

from left: Niki (Chis's big sister), Alana who lived in the neighbourhood; Peter and his best friend Bob, Voula, Theo Hadis, Jimmy, Steven Hadis, Cousin Peter, Peggy and John Hadis

Voula in grade 4 with Peter in grade 3. They are standing beside the stump of the palm tree mentioned in Chapter 20. Bob's house is in the background.

the shelter sheds

Chapter 13
Fun, Games and Pets

Often, migrant families share a house until they can save up a bit of money to rent on their own or until they can afford their own place. This was the case when Theo sponsored his younger brother, George, who arrived in Hamilton in February of 1961. George was married with a child, a son, Peter. Another Peter? Well it is a cultural tradition, that sons name their own sons and daughters after *their* parents. *Peter* had been the name of Theo's and George's father and this was their way of honouring him and continuing his name. In order to differentiate between the two Peters, one was called Peter T, after Theo, and the other Peter G, after George. Over time however, Peter T became just plain Peter, but for his cousin, the name Peter G stuck for life! They both enjoyed the same things; both had strong personalities and both were about the same age. Cousin Peter G and his parents lived with Argyro and Theo for a couple of years until they had saved up enough money to buy their own house in Goldsmith Street, only a block away, down Billy Goat Hill.

Not many people in Australia had televisions before the mid-60s, so what did the two Peters, and other children, do in a small town to pass the time? Obviously they made up their own games! For example, the Peters used to like playing with toy cars. One day Peter's parents bought him a tin fire-engine that was about 30 centimetres long. They also gave one exactly the same to Peter G. Consequently, the two Peters spent many happy hours together making roads in the dirt for their engines to zoom around on.

One particular day, the two Peters were happily playing in the old garage, located in the back yard. One of the fire engine trucks got dented and no one was sure exactly how it happened. Peter claimed that it was his cousin's truck that was damaged, while Peter G insisted that his own truck was the undamaged one. So they had a big fight. Tempers flared! Both boys were red-faced with anger.

Suddenly, Peter grabbed the undamaged truck with the intention of dashing out of the old garage. That was too much for his cousin, Peter G, to bear. Feeling desperate because he was about to lose his beloved truck, Peter G took decisive action. In the garage there were some tools, including an old, rusty saw. He grabbed the saw and slammed it into the top of Peter's head! Ouch!! Peter instantly let go of the truck he was holding, to grab his sore head and to feel his wounds. His head was throbbing and blood was pouring onto his hair, over his face and down his neck and shoulders. Forgetting about the wonderful firetruck, he ran into the house to find his mother and get help. Voula ran after him; she had witnessed the whole thing. They found Argyro in the kitchen cooking lunch for her kids and humming a Greek tune to herself, "Asta ta malakia sou anakatomena...".

Well! You can imagine the shock on poor Argyro's face! In the one breath she let out a cry of shock and also asked what had happened. Simultaneously, she frantically searched in her son's hair to locate the wound. On his scalp she saw a row of neat holes made by the teeth of the saw. Unfortunately, they were quite deep and bled profusely! From the amount of blood and the fact that she knew the saw was rusty, Argyro realised it could be serious with the potential of becoming infected. She had to act quickly.

Since she didn't have a car, she called out from her kitchen window to her neighbour, Margaret Shmitz. When Margaret hung her head out of her window, Argyro asked her to ring for a taxi to take them to the hospital. Next she pushed a clean tea towel onto Peter's head and held it there. Then they went outside to wait for the taxi, which arrived very quickly since Hamilton was only 3 km at its widest point. The doctor put ten stitches in Peter's scalp, gave him a tetanus injection and sent him home to rest! Cousin Peter got a smack on his bottom for his mischief and was warned against fighting again! Peter remained indoors for a few days under the watchful eye of his mother. The two Peters ended up together: reading, playing with their marbles or organising armies with their little green plastic soldiers. Sometimes they laughed and sometimes they argued. Life was back to normal again!

Voula also experienced some unpalatable little "incidents". One winter evening she was playing near the kitchen wood-fed, iron stove, enjoying the warmth it radiated. On top it had flat, iron plates that were heated by the fire below. Argyro would put her pots and pans onto these to cook the family meals. Underneath and to the right was an oven while at the bottom was a long drawer where damp pieces of wood could be placed to dry out, ready to feed the fire. During that particular evening, Voula opened the bottom drawer so the family's kitten could get in and warm itself up, as was its habit. Unfortunately she forgot about the kitten and someone closed the drawer, not realising the kitten was still asleep inside. Therefore, the next day when Argyro bent over to see if there was some dry wood in the drawer, she found a nasty surprise! What could she do? It was too late to do anything! How sad the kids were for it had been their favourite kitten; so playful and friendly. However, there were several other kittens around at that time, so it was only mourned for a short time.

Mother Cat was always busy either having a litter of kittens or caring for them. She gave birth twice or thrice a year! The children learnt they mustn't touch baby kittens if they were too young to open their eyes. If they did touch them, then the kittens would get infected with pus in their eyes, become very sick and die. They had to be patient and wait for the kittens to grow and to be able to use their eyes. Then they would be strong enough to stay alive when they were played with. Unfortunately, sometimes they found the kittens so cute they couldn't resist holding them–for just a little while. If they did that, then the inevitable happened: the kittens eventually died even after being so greatly loved!

Well, Voula often played around the stove on cold evenings, because it felt so warm and cosy to stand nearby; there was no other heating in the house besides the log fire-place in the lounge room which was not always lit. On one occasion she was jumping up and down next to the stove when she suddenly tripped. To save herself from falling, she had a split second to react and was forced to put the palm of her hand on one of the hot iron plates to push her body away from the stove. She saved her face and chest from being burned, but her poor palm, just under her thumb, felt very hot and sore. Her mother put it under cold water and then put butter on it. In those days everyone thought that was the thing to do. However, when Voula woke up the following morning she saw something that horrified her! A burn blister had grown overnight. Not just a small blister but a huge blister! It was the size of a small *egg*!

Voula felt like an alien. What would the kids at school think of her now? They would tease her for sure and call her a freak. Kids can be cruel sometimes when someone is different and Voula was already different because her parents were migrants. Anyway she tried to hide it with a Band-Aid but it didn't cover much. The blister could still be seen very clearly under and around the Band-Aid, so Voula kept her hand behind her back or hid it up her sleeve, or in a pocket. She got quite good at hiding it until she was put out of her misery one day when she accidentally fell on the wet bathroom floor and the blister burst! It had felt so good after it burst and the pain was gone! Voula wondered why she hadn't thought of popping it herself. Her hand was normal again. What a relief!

On one occasion Argyro had allowed Voula to watch a TV show, "Combat" starring Vic Morrow. It showed muddy soldiers shooting the enemy during WW2. There were no gory scenes, just dirty soldiers. There was an interesting scene where the soldiers used petrol and poured it along the road towards an enemy truck. Then they hid far away and threw a match on the poured petrol. Voula was amazed to see a fiery trail travelling quickly towards the truck and then…KABOOM! That scene played in her mind for days, until she was tempted to experiment with some petrol that was used for the lawn mower. Voula knew exactly where it was stored in the outside laundry. She took the small cap off the petrol can and poured some petrol into the cap. Where could she put it for safety? She didn't want to burn down the laundry! The two laundry troughs were made of concrete. Surely the concrete was enough to prevent any damage from a small volume of burning petrol?! She carefully placed the cap of petrol onto the base of a trough. Then Voula had trouble lighting a match, but finally succeeded. She only had a moment to hold the match in the air, about a foot from the cap, before dropping it with a cry of fear. The petrol had ignited and flamed up through the air, singeing her fringe, eyelashes and eyebrows. Voula learned first-hand the meaning of "highly flammable." The little girl ran into the house to find her mother and after a few hurried explanations and checking that there were no burns, Argyro smacked her daughter's bottom, for being naughty and playing with petrol. She told her to learn her lesson and not to do anything like that again!

However, Argyro herself was not guiltless of foolish little actions, or of the necessity of learning from her own mistakes. There was not much awareness of animal welfare in the 1960s, and being raised in a rural community Argyro's attitude towards animals was very pragmatic. She got sick and tired of Mother Cat constantly having litters and litters of kittens and decided to get rid of her! She put the cat in a box together with her most recent litter of kittens and asked Mr. Hadis to drive her to the country-side outside Hamilton. There, they placed the box beside some trees and drove home. Feral cats were not part of national awareness and this type of thing was not unusual behaviour back then.

Oblivious of what had happened, Voula called for Mother Cat every day, to feed her, "Here puss, puss, puss!" but it was futile. Then one day, a strange cat appeared. It was haggard and so lean, Voula could see the outline of its bones through its fur. Voula brought out some milk in a saucer, but the cat was distrustful of humans and it waited until Voula backed away, before coming to the saucer to lap up the milk. Voula went to tell her mother but when Argyro came out to see, the cat had gone.

A few days later it returned, and this time Argyro saw it. With a shock she realised it was Mother Cat, who had found her way back home! Argyro felt deep remorse and guilt at the sight of the poor cat. They say confession is good for the soul, and Argyro had no choice but to "fess-up," telling her kids what she had done and vowing never to try to do away with their pets ever again. Never again did Mother Cat trust people and never again did Argyro behave with unkindness towards an animal. Well, except for when some of her hens would become "clucky" and stop laying, only to sit on eggs that would never hatch. To start the chooks laying eggs again, Argyro employed certain methods, that she had picked up from her village life in Greece, and it was effective but not pleasant.

The dented fire truck became Jimmy's favourite toy.

Peter G and his mum are with Voula, Peter and Jimmy.

Theo with his brother George

Sitting on their swing are: Cousin Theo from Melbourne, Peter holding Mother Cat, Peter G holding Ginger and Jimmy holding a toy car.

Chapter 14
At Home

During the weekends the family carried on as usual: the parents continued to work, Theo in the Cafe every weekday and half a day on Saturdays and Argyro tried to organise and clean her home. When it got busy in the cafe, during lunch hour, Argyro helped out as a waitress. She became so proficient at handling plates; she could balance three plates on each arm. It was amazing to see!

Since Argyro had limited time, Voula was often told to vacuum and do the beds because she was *a girl and had to learn about housework*. Also, as Argyro often reminded her, she would be a good wife and mother one day. Even though Voula resented the curbing of her natural desire to be outside enjoying nature, she often had to help her mother, but usually it was under duress.

Argyro took the training of her only daughter very seriously and over the years, systematically instructed Voula to water the garden, vacuum the house, sew, knit, cook family meals and bake. Voula's sultana cakes became popular in her family and Mrs Hadis wanted her daughter Peggy to learn to make this cake too. So one day Voula walked down Billy Goat Hill to visit Peggy and make a cake with her. She was shocked as she arrived at Peggy's back gate for there, running around the back yard was a headless chook, chased by Mr Hadis! The rooster had been pecking his hens and now it was going to become the family's dinner! (After that Voula didn't feel like eating chicken for a very long time.)

She escaped into the house and found herself in the kitchen with Peggy and Mrs Hadis, who was preparing ingredients, and encouraging Voula to make a start: a great compliment for a young girl. They used fresh eggs for the cake because the Hadis' family chooks were great layers!

One of Voula's greatest upsets to her house-keeping, was when the boys, Peter and his best friend Bob, would take a short-cut to the back yard by walking through the front door, and along the passageway to get out the back door! They could easily have walked around either side of the house but no, they couldn't be bothered! They usually walked through the house wearing their dirty boots, leaving muddy prints all over Voula's vacuumed, crimson carpet!! Argh! Voula complained bitterly to them when they did this, by running to the front door just in time to lecture them. It did no good, as boys will be boys. They didn't want her to think she could lord it over them so they ignored her and marched on through anyway.

This was how Voula got the reputation of being "bossy." You see she didn't give up trying to *teach* the boys that they shouldn't walk through the house in their dirty shoes. Sometimes they took pity on her and held their boots aloft in their hands, in a teasing manner, but Voula always felt it was because she had badgered them into it and not because they had finally learnt some common courtesy! However, it wasn't only Voula battling to get some appreciation and "house break" the boys. On one occasion Peter earned the ire of his mother because of his antics! It happened that Peter had been watching "The Lone Ranger" on the telly (about a masked cowboy and his Indian friend who helped people in trouble). The Lone Ranger was a "goody" and Peter admired him a lot. In particular, he was fascinated by the way the Lone Ranger could jump from a high window or from a balcony, and land on his saddle on his horse! The Lone Ranger often whistled for his horse to come to him, and then he would jump onto his horse and make a "quick getaway" to escape from the "crooks" trying to shoot him.

That morning Peter had parked his bike under the kitchen window, which was about one and a half metres from the ground. After having his breakfast of scrambled eggs, he said goodbye to his mother and suddenly surprised her by climbing out the window, just above his beloved bike. Argyro, was completely taken aback, but quickly recovered from her amazement and ordered him back inside. At that moment Argyro noticed that Mrs Shmitz, the neighbour, was having a sticky-beak out of her window and Argyro felt ashamed of what she might be thinking.

Peter was in a cheeky mood and ignoring his mother, actually cheered for himself and climbed down onto his *bike saddle* for a "quick getaway". Peter thought to himself, "This is just like the Lone Ranger!" Argyro was very upset because he had refused to obey her and seemed to think the whole thing was a lot of fun. She also did think of it as quite a funny situation, but she reached for the nearest missile available to her: it was a fresh egg. Taking quick aim, she landed it on top of Peter's head just before he took off, "splat!" It left a gooey mess in his hair, which she of course had to help him wash out. After that he was forbidden to make a "quick getaway" and only succumbed to the temptation when he thought his mother wouldn't see him!

Having studied dressmaking in Athens, Argyro was an excellent seamstress so she often made lovely clothes for her only daughter. Voula's dresses were full skirted, often lacy and very feminine. One of her favourite dresses was worn to Sunday

School at the local Church of Christ (there were no Greek Orthodox churches in Hamilton so that's where the kids went to Sunday School). It was a pastel pink with a wide fabric belt tied in a bow at the back. By the time Voula got back from church, lunch was on the table, so she usually didn't change out of her "Sunday Best" till later. After lunch she often forgot, couldn't be bothered, or just wanted to keep wearing her favourite dress. This was a big mistake!

One Sunday after lunch, she went outside to play *Cowboys and Indians* with Jimmy and Peter. The boys decided that they would be the cowboys and Voula would be the Indian. They gave her a flimsy, plastic bow and some small arrows with which to shoot them. Then, to make it "equitable", they told her they were going to shoot at her with water from the garden hose, because their guns didn't actually shoot anything. "That's not fair!" declared poor Voula as she raced to turn off the tap. Peter warned her to keep away from it or he would use the water hose on her. Then he jeeringly aimed the hose at his sister. She stood akimbo, calling his bluff. "You wouldn't dare wet my best dress," Voula confronted Peter angrily. The next thing she knew, cold water was soaking through her dress and onto her skin! Voula yelled in frustration, but Peter kept squirting until Voula ran away to tell her mother. It was hard for Voula to accept what Argyro told her, "Don't play with boys. It serves you right!" Consequently, Voula was even more angry and distressed than ever! She felt there was no justice in the world!

Another example of playful "boyish" fun was the time the boys practised their footy jumps and ball kicking skills in their bedroom. Often Peter and Jimmy fell on the walls, floor and beds with loud thumps and bumps. Sometimes the ball hit their bedroom window and broke it. Over time, they learnt to use "soft balls" because of the large number of warnings issued by their mother: they practised their drop-kicks by using a large bundled ball of socks. As there were quite a few socks used to form the "ball" it was actually fairly heavy and when Peter drop-kicked it to Jimmy on the other side of their bedroom, it accidentally flew into the window-pane and broke the glass again! (This window was actually broken several times.)

We know a woman's work is never done, and Argyro had to very painstakingly vacuum and re-vacuum her sons' room to ensure no glass slivers would enter their bare feet–there seemed to be millions of them everywhere! Also their beds had to be changed too and the sheets and blankets shaken out. For several weeks she kept finding broken glass in the boys' carpet just when she thought she had got it all. When would the boys learn to be more careful?

The Lone Ranger with his faithful side-kick, Tonto and Silver, his horse.

from left: Peter, Voula, Jimmy and Bob in the Botanical Gardens

Chapter 15
Obsessions and Hobbies

After Jimmy's accident, there were no more unfortunate events, but Voula pondered on the accident and tried to understand *why* it had happened. Why Jimmy? Why *her* family? This is a question common to all humans at some point in their lives. Why, why, why did bad things happen? Most times there is no answer to this common question about fate. She asked her mother and Argyro replied that it had just been bad luck and that, sometimes, these things happened in life. A sensible response.

Voula became obsessed with preventing any bad luck from befalling her family after Jimmy's accident. Was there anything she could do to ward off evil and ensure good fortune? She began to take notice of other people's superstitions like: if you blow out all your birthday candles your wish will come true; never walk under a ladder, and according to her teacher, some people thought that breaking a mirror would bring seven years of bad luck! Then Voula realised she was not the only one concerned with warding off misfortune. Others had tackled this issue before her, and had thoughtfully made some rules for people to follow! For example, if you spill salt out of a saltshaker, get a pinch of salt and throw it over your left shoulder to reverse bad fortune!

On a certain day, as Voula, Peter and Jimmy were walking to school, Voula happened to notice a caterpillar on a tree by the side of the footpath. She stopped to study it and walked around the tree for a better view. Then she hurried to catch up with her brothers. Suddenly a thought electrified Voula and she stopped in her tracks. Everything had been going well in her life since the accident, but what if her *deviation from her regular walk to school* would effect future events for the worse? Could her behaviour influence fate? Was it good luck versus bad luck? Was it just coincidence that everything was going well with her family or was it some pattern of behaviour that brought good luck? What if her walk around the tree, which had been different from her usual behaviour, created a different future: bad luck might result? She raced back to the tree and circled around it to the side she would normally go past and then walked at a normal speed, back to her brothers.

After that she noticed some other things like an uneven crack in the footpath and decided it would be bad luck to step on it. When she crossed the road, she decided to walk north and then turn west, not west first and then north. On the return trip, she felt she had to walk in the exact opposite direction in order to "undo" the movements she had done in the morning. Her fear of jinxing herself and her family extended to other careful rituals, like where she walked first in her bedroom and second and third… Day after day, week after week, Voula followed strict movements and felt trapped, bound by her own superstitions of bad luck. She didn't know she was suffering from psychological obsessive behaviour, Obsessive Compulsive Disorder.

Being the eldest child in the family, she felt all the responsibility and (let it be said) pride of her position. Not in a million years would she want her siblings to get a whiff of what she was doing. She knew she was being irrational and felt ashamed to let anyone know about her behaviour, so she took care to walk behind Peter at the right places, to avoid his knowing what she was up to. However, one day as they were walking home, Peter asked her, "Why do you always walk around that tree clockwise and then anticlockwise?" Voula was vague, "I want to," was her response. Peter told her he thought she was being silly and did stupid things. Voula's secret was out! She noticed Peter watching her and to prove him wrong, she avoided her obsessive movements and even walked on the crack on the footpath!

The next few days Peter watched Voula carefully and Voula watched Peter too. If he was watching she didn't follow her superstitions. After some time, she realised that nothing "bad" had happened and she was cured. Sometimes she had a relapse, but gradually she forgot about her obsession with warding off bad luck. It is not always as easy as that, for people who suffer an obsessive compulsion, to stop behaving in a bizarre way. In the 1960s, people often became obsessed with a hobby. During their leisure time, some people would be consumed by collecting things like: coins, dolls, spoons and plates: anything really. Others just enjoyed a hobby as a diversion, for fun and didn't go *overboard*! Argyro, having siblings in Greece, received mail with Greek stamps on the envelopes, so she used it as an opportunity to educate Voula about Greece, Hellas. The stamps often portrayed the Greek royal family, heroes from mythology and the ancient Greek gods.

Argyro showed her daughter how to remove the stamps by soaking them in cold water until they could be easily peeled off the envelopes. Then they were allowed to dry and then put in her album. Most stamp albums had names of countries on different blank pages where the collector could paste their stamps.

However, Voula's album had open rows of clear plastic for the stamps to be placed into. The stamps could easily be rearranged and moved about, but there were no headings for countries.

Argyro encouraged Voula to collect *used* stamps rather than buying packets of unused stamps from the post office. Argyro believed these stamps were more *authentic*. It was a slow process until Auntie Tasia from Greece heard that Voula was starting a stamp collection. Tasia was eleven years older than Voula and had just graduated as a secondary school teacher. She generously sent Voula most of her own stamps in her next letter to Australia and Voula started to enthusiastically organise her stamps. She was very seriously stuck on stamp collecting for several months. She thought Auntie Tasia was very kind and must love her very much, to give up her own stamps to her niece like that! The Australian stamps were had from bills and letters from Argyro's sister in Melbourne and a cousin from Adelaide. They were five cents and the queen looked very young and beautiful.

Voula's favourite stamps, because of their distinctive shapes, were an Egyptian stamp, which had sixteen sides, and a stamp from the Gabonese Republic, which was triangular. She hoped that one day they would be worth a fortune! Anyhow, Voula was dreaming, because she was not dedicated to stamp collecting, and her interest lasted only a couple of years. According to Confucius, the Chinese philosopher, it does not matter how slowly you go, so long as you don't stop. As it was, Voula lost interest in her stamp collection and, on a positive note, thank God she didn't become obsessive about stamps!

Theo and his family are holding Greek-style Easter eggs: the red hard-boiled ones. It is just seven months after Jimmy's accident on 25/4/1965.

After Jimmy's accident, Voula wanted to stop bad luck from happening to her family.

Chapter 16
The Woodshed

In the back yard, there was a laundry, a garage, an outhouse, and an adjoining woodshed. The shed was about two and a half metres wide and long and maybe two metres high. Its walls were made of old fence palings with gaps between them, and it had a flat corrugated iron roof. Peter, being adventurous, soon learnt to climb on this roof and then as he got older he could jump off it onto the long, spongy pile of grass below. From the shed roof he could also climb onto the higher corrugated roof of the garage. Whenever a ball got on the roof, Peter would climb up and retrieve it.

In order to provide fuel for the kitchen stove, chunks of wood were placed on a stump in an upright position and then chopped with an axe into smaller pieces that could fit into its burner. Under supervision, Voula was allowed to chop wood as she got older and stronger.

One day the kids were playing Hidey. Someone decided to climb over the stacked and loose lying wood, into the woodshed: it may have been Peter or maybe it was his best friend, Bob. Anyway, Peter, Bob and Jimmy hid inside the woodshed, surrounded by chunks of wood for walls and Voula couldn't find them. It was a really ingenious hiding place! This game was repeated over the next few weeks and then, while passing the woodshed, Voula heard some voices: the boys were *inside* the woodshed! When she tried to get in, she found her way barred by a wall of piled chunks of wood. The boys had stacked it against the walls of the shed and left a hollow place in the middle for a little room, where they could relax. Inside they had moved a few pieces of wood to be chairs and a table. They even had three glasses of soft drink and some of their footy cards to look at. Now they were in the middle of a game of Monopoly! Voula was amazed, as well as impressed.

When the boys heard her moving some of the timber wall at the front, they moved away some of the wood from the back wall of the shed and escaped through a gap in the paling fence of the shed. Then they walked along between the neighbour's fence and the back of the shed and garage, over the top of the garden rubbish, bottles and corrugated iron off-cuts that had been dumped there. They got away from Voula but she had finally discovered their hiding place!

When Argyro heard about her children building a room in the woodshed, she lost it! She told them that it was too dangerous and that the timber could fall on them and hurt or kill them. They were strictly forbidden to enter the shed again. So for a long time the kids avoided the shed, although Voula often walked past and looked at it very thoughtfully.

A little time later, the Hidey game was on again and besides hiding in some of the garden bushes, Voula ran out of ideas. The boys had sticks that they used to poke into the bushes and one exciting time Peter just missed putting his stick onto Voula's back, but he hadn't found her! Voula had looked right into Pete's eyes and felt sure he had seen her! Amazingly, he kept moving along poking here and there, and she was glad she had remained calm and hadn't rushed out of her hiding place to escape the boys. They were getting frustrated searching for her and were being careless, so it would have been better for them to give it up entirely! The boys soon moved away to the front of the woodshed, calling out that if she was in there, they would tell on her and she would be in trouble. They even climbed in and had a look but Voula was not there. When her brothers went around to the front of the house to look there, she quickly raced out of her hiding spot in the bush, and carefully climbed over the piles of wood and into the woodshed. She made it safer and more stable by quietly moving the wood around, and then she remained there for ages.

When the boys got bored and gave up looking for her, she went into the house to find them. "Where have *you* been?" they quizzed her, but she staunchly refused to tell them. The woodshed was forbidden, so of course she didn't want to shed any light on *that*! She now had a fantastic secret hiding place that she enjoyed keeping to herself. Voula wouldn't tell about the woodshed, no matter how often they asked her! Whenever she was upset and felt like crying, she hid in there until she felt better. At other times Voula just enjoyed the smell of the wood and the earth, and having her own private place to herself. She especially relished it when it rained, and she could hear the noisy rain falling on the corrugated iron roof: it was very loud, but somehow, comforting. Mothers can't watch their children twenty-four seven, and it was sheer luck that Voula escaped injury in the woodshed, when a wall of stacked timber collapsed around her and she jumped out of the way only squashing her shoe.

Another game, of *Find the Treasure*, was invented by someone in the neighbourhood and Peter and Bob were keen to play it again, so they showed Voula, Jimmy, Peggy and her brothers. The game was thrilling, exciting and time consuming. There had to be two teams, a prize and a time limit. The seeking team had to stay at home for 15 minutes and not look outside: it was an honesty system which didn't always work very well. Then the other team used a piece of chalk to draw arrows, in difficult to find places that once found would lead the seeking team to the "treasure": usually a comestible, like a block of chocolate. The game involved a one kilometre radius or so, around the block of houses and could last a couple of hours. It was very exciting and Prince, the family dog, usually tagged along too. If the seeking team was good at finding the clues and caught up with the other team, they all had to run back home and the first team back were the winners. But it was a bit of a shemozzle for the whole of one team to return home before the other, as the littler children couldn't run as fast. If however, the seekers couldn't find the treasure then the other team ate it themselves. That happened a lot!

The dilapidated woodshed can be seen in the background on the left, along with the grassy heap Peter would jump onto to get off the roof of the shed.

Chapter 17
The Hamilton Show

Being a rural city centre, Hamilton prides itself on all its agricultural products, but especially on the high quality of its sheep. It claims the title of "Current Wool Capital of the World". Originally coming from Spain, the Merino sheep, unlike many of the other European animals imported to Australia, thrived, because it could cope with the Australian heat. Whereas Australia relies on the housing market and on coal and steel exports to bolster its economy, it was not so in past years. The economy used to depend on "the sheep's back", since the wool industry prospered and we exported our fine wool to ready overseas markets.

Merinos are known for their superior, thick fleece, which is highly suitable for making into a fine fibre, and is mainly used in clothing. As mentioned, farmers in the Western District of Victoria, of which Hamilton is the capital city, are very proud of their agriculture and animals. To that end, they formed the Hamilton Pastoral and Agricultural Society. The Society held the Hamilton Show every year. It was for showing farm animals and for sharing farming ideas about their produce. Shows in city centers are still popular in Australia, but are more for entertainment and business information than for helping farmers meet up and exchange ideas. Nowadays, the *Hamilton Show* has been renamed *Sheepvention*: a blended word, combining "sheep" and "convention". Every year, Sheepvention is a two-day event held at the Hamilton Showgrounds on Shakespeare Street. It holds sheep sales, competitions and fashions, as well as entertainment.

Back in the 1960s, Jimmy, Peter and Voula were always very excited to go to the Hamilton Show, because there were many interesting things to see there. It had a carnival atmosphere just like you get in the big cities during the Royal Melbourne Show or the Sydney Royal Easter Show. It was all about sheep, cows, fashion, games, jam and cake competitions. Also, there were sheep dog competitions, to select the dog that could most quickly and gently group sheep together and direct them into a pen. Very popular were the wood chopping competitions, in which men used axes to determine who was the fastest to chop his log. There were the usual stalls like the carnival clown heads, windmills and Kewpie dolls on sticks and free showbags. Whenever the kids put the balls in the clown's mouth, they could never get them to go into the big numbers to win a large stuffed toy. The timing was always wrong and the balls sometimes got stuck and slowed down. It was always just bad luck! The windmills were better value for money because they lasted longer. The kids would spin around to create "wind" and watch the windmill spin fast. Eventually it would get loose and fall off its stick. However, the best value of all were the Kewpie dolls because Argyro liked them and kept them in her bedroom, on her vanity, as decorations because they had colourful, glittery dresses. Voula was forbidden to play with them, but she could still admire them in her mother's bedroom.

One year the family paid to go inside a tent with the banner "Samson the Strongman". Inside was tiered, wooden seating and the ground was covered with sawdust. The audience noticed there was a group of people facing the seating. Among them was Samson, dressed in an old-fashioned bathing costume, and when he was introduced, everyone clapped. He started the performance by holding up some razor blades and warning his audience NEVER to try to copy him. Samson then put the blades into his mouth and started chewing them. Voula felt sick! His tongue must be bleeding. "Please spit them out!" she willed him. But no, Samson kept on chewing and finally swallowed the razor blades! One of the audience was asked to come forward and look into his mouth. Well it seemed the blade was eaten up, but maybe it was a trick. After all, what the eyes see, the heart believes!

Next, a platform of sharp nails was brought in from the back of the tent and Samson walked over and lay on top of it. A man was asked to volunteer from the audience and he was handed a sledge hammer. A piece of timber was placed over Samson and then a large rock on top of the timber.

The volunteer was asked to hit the rock and break it. Samson held his breath and tightened his muscles but otherwise made no sound. The repeated banging of the sledgehammer reverberated on the rock until it broke. Once the rock and timber were removed from Samson's belly, he stood up and shook hands, thanking the volunteer and assuring him he was okay. Next thing you know, Samson lay back on the bed of nails and a car was driven on top of him. It was all too much!! Voula just wanted to get out of there. Just as well it was the highlight of the performance and then everyone began filing out soon afterwards. But Argyro was proud to learn Samson was a Greek and she insisted on taking her children over to meet him. It remained indelibly printed on their minds and they never forgot Samson—the strong man. (For more information and a video about Samson refer to : http://www.abc.net.au/news/2015-06-01/car-eating-strongman-samson-reclaims-family-and-showbiz-legacy/6507660)

A favourite attraction was the Scottish dancing. You could stand next to a wooden platform that rested on four giant drums. As a bagpiper, dressed in a Scottish kilt, started up his bagpipes, pretty girls, also dressed in kilts, stepped up onto the platform. The girls looked very exotic in their tartan kilts. On their family tartan skirts representing their ancestry, they wore lovely decorative pins. When the bagpipe music reached the correct place the girls would begin to dance. Often they placed two swords on the platform so they criss-crossed one another. Then they deftly danced over the swords with upright bodies. Such was their skill they did not trip or touch the swords once! While they danced and jumped in the air, the platform creaked and bounced. They wore pumps on their feet similar to ballerinas and they were very nimble, pointing their toes and holding their hands and fingers up in the air. Sometimes the girls danced alone and at other times in pairs or more. The best dancers won first prize, usually a blue ribbon. It was all very beautiful and of course Voula felt inspired that maybe she could take some ballet lessons and grow up to be a ballerina some day!

The Hamilton Show, 1911
Creator: George Walker Museum Victoria http://collections.museumvictoria.com.au/items/766724

Hamilton still prides itself on being the current wool capital of the world.

Merino sheep

Chapter 18
Going for Sunday Drives

It was Sunday and a beautiful, sunny day with a clear blue sky. It is an Aussie tradition to go for a Sunday drive, so Andy Hadis and Theo decided to visit their Greek friends who also ran a cafe, in Portland on the southern coastline of Victoria. They would discuss work and perhaps ask them how their business was affected by the hotels now offering "counter-lunches." Lucas Cafe felt it was going nowhere in the future, as it had lost business to the pubs that had begun to serve lunches, so maybe it would help to get their heads together.

Andy had a 1956 Holden he had named Spiro, so he would drive their two families to the seaside town. It would take about an hour and a half down the Henty Highway, which is named after the man who first settled in the Portland area with his family, Edward Henty, in 1834. He tilled the land and grew the first wheat crop too. As Melbourne was first founded by John Batman in 1835, you see Portland was the first European settlement in Victoria.

Theo sat in the passenger seat and their wives in the back. Between them they had seven small children who sat beside them in the front seat and in the back seat. It was very squashy, but they managed to fit on the bench seats, because there were no seat belts and the smaller children sat on the laps of the bigger ones.

As they travelled along, they could see lots of rubbish that had been thrown out of car windows. The road was littered with bags, empty cigarette packets and glass bottles. During the first half of the 20th century, people had a different mind-set and did not really concern themselves about pollution. It was not until 1969 that a major anti-littering movement, "Keep Australia Beautiful," began in Australia with slogans like, "Do the right thing" and "Tidy Towns."

Portland is about 85km from Hamilton, so when they arrived there, the children felt stiff and restless. They wanted to run free, so out they went to play along the beach. Voula was having fun running on the sand and grassy area. She took off her shoes and socks and felt the cool sand between her toes. It felt good. She didn't see the bee in the grass until she stepped on it and it had stung her. She yelped with pain. Argyro took the stinger out but her foot was sore, red and swollen. They went to their friend's cafe for ice! Voula could not run for the rest of the day and was miserable, sitting with ice on her foot while the adults talked.

Another time Theo and Andy drove to Portland, Theo took his daughter along as well, for an outing. She sat in the back seat behind her father. It was all going very nicely with a few songs sung along the way, when eventually, Theo decided to have a cigarette. He lit up and threw the dead match out of the window. To spare Andy the work of emptying out the car's ash tray, Theo also flicked his cigarette ash out of his window. Voula had opened her window to aerate the car, because she hated breathing in the smoke from her dad's cigarettes. Unfortunately, Theo's cigarette ash flew back into the car through Voula's window and got onto her clothes. Voula looked down and saw some sparks had started burning holes in her collar. As she cried out for help, Andy stopped the car on the side of the road and Theo jumped out to check his daughter. He smothered the sparks and double checked that they were truly extinguished. Theo looked a bit startled and didn't smoke in the car after that.

Port Fairy and Warrnambool were also favourite destinations for the families, but again it was always in hot and cramped conditions, with everyone sitting on top of each other. At Warrnambool, the Twelve Apostles were a terrific sight (even though there were only nine of them!) and the rocks together with the rock pools were fun to scamper over. Along the cliffs were many fossils of marine creatures, so fossicking with a little pick or a strong stone was another popular pastime.

About 16km west of Hamilton are the Wannon Falls and to the north of Hamilton, about 77km and an hour and twenty minutes away, are the Grampians, with hundreds of steps leading down to amazing waterfalls and rocks. It was unusual if someone did not fall or get injured, as the children ran excitedly from one place to another. They were thrilled by the thunderous noise of the waterfalls and enjoyed the cool water on their toes, after scurrying around on the rocks in the sunshine.

Argyro holding Jimmy, at the Falls

Mrs Hadis and Argyro with their children at Wannon Falls

Chapter 19
Guy Fawkes Night

All the neighbours were collecting their garden rubbish. They were making a big heap outside Theo's house, on the road. It was Guy Fawkes' night, or Bonfire Night, November 5, and everyone was bringing wood and dry branches to put on the heap of rubbish on the road. All the children were very excited, so all afternoon they helped very energetically. One of the men took control and made sure no one put anything on the heap that would smell: like old rubber tyres.

Someone made a life-size effigy of Guy Fawkes out of paper and old clothes. There was even an old hat on its head! Guy Fawkes was the man who had tried to blow up the Houses of Parliament in England, back in 1605 and was sentenced to death for his crime. So why were country folk, in Australia, in 1968, celebrating the death of Guy Fawkes? Well it was something that many Australians celebrated back in the 1960s because of Australia's British origins. The children didn't understand about Guy Fawkes until they were older, but they enjoyed the excitement and the feeling of community with all the neighbours.

By the time evening came around, everyone had gathered together to watch the bonfire. Furthermore, this was "Cracker Night" so people brought along their fireworks, which they had bought from the Milk Bar down the road: it was legal in those days for shops to sell them. All the boys wanted to throw crackers into the bonfire: the bigger, the better! The big "Penny Bungers" were the loudest and therefore the most popular!

However, Voula preferred the "sparklers" the best. She liked to hold a sparkler and wave it around, pretending she was a fairy princess.

As you may imagine, Peter, Voula's younger brother, had a different plan and it involved his Penny Bungers. His best friend Bob Tydon lived across the road, and together they liked to put a tin can over a Penny Bunger, light the fuse and run away. After a few moments a big "boom" was heard and the tin can went flying into the sky. A bit dangerous you might say, but lots of kids did things like that in their back yards in those years. Everyone had big blocks of land, of at least a quarter of an acre. The can usually didn't go over the fence, but if it did Peter and Bob would scramble over the fence, like a pair of wild goats, and quickly retrieve their special can, ready for repeat explosions.

As Voula was often left to herself, because the boys didn't want to play with a girl, she found ways to amuse herself. She had discovered that there were seventeen ant nests in her back yard! She got it in her head that she should take care of them. After all, they were in *her* yard and someone had to look after them and make life more pleasant for them! She used to get a slice of bread and wander about making tiny crumbs for the ants to find. In order to save them time and trouble she visited the entrance of each nest and there she would leave her gift of breadcrumbs.

Voula was sure the ants appreciated it because she lay still on the ground for hours, carefully watching them. When the crumb was first discovered, the foraging ant that found it got very excited. Often it tried to move the crumb by itself, but if it couldn't, it would go and get help. Ants really know how to work well together! In no time at all there was a black line of ants running quickly up and down to their new food source. Sometimes the ants had a war with other insects and then they often carried their baby lava out of their nest to safety. Voula spent many happy hours following them to their new nests and learning their behaviour. Sometimes she got involved in their wars by trying to find and kill their enemies. Unfortunately, she didn't see the ants' biggest enemy. It was Peter!

One particular day, soon after Guy Fawkes, Peter decided it would be fun to blow up ant nests with some crackers he had left over from Cracker Night! Unlike his sister, Pete thought ants were uninteresting and inconsequential in the garden, and it would be great to see a little explosion of a cracker in an ant hole. He used up all his crackers blowing them up and then, when he ran out of them he used the hose and flooded their homes! His best mate Bob was his accomplice and they were having a wonderful time together.

When his sister saw the carnage, she was very upset with Pete and they had a big fight, but it was too late. Most of the poor ants were dead! Voula thought that they had died just because she had made pets of them, and that if she had left them alone Peter would not have noticed them and contrived his wicked plan! Fortunately, he had not found all the nests and Voula was careful to feed them secretly, when her brother was not around, so as not to draw attention to them. She held a grudge against him for several days and then Argyro told her ants were a nuisance and that Voula shouldn't feed them and encourage more of them in the garden. Is that true though? In the end, Voula forgave Pete. What else could she do?

Chapter 20
Pets

Most children love animals and Argyro's and Theo's children were no exception. Since Voula was often excluded by the boys, animals were her playmates and friends. Many fulfilling hours were spent watching, training and learning the behaviour of these interesting creatures. Like many other families who lived in the country at that time, they had a small menagerie of pets, which included Mother Cat, who was always having litters of kittens, because she had never been spayed. A rather attractive offspring of Mother Cat was Ginger, named for his orange fur.

Voula loved watching "Lassie" on TV. Lassie was a very intelligent, friendly family dog that rescued her human family whenever they got into trouble. Also, it was fascinating to watch Lassie obey commands like "sit," "come," "stay," and many other things. The family didn't have a dog yet, and Voula longed for a dog she could walk around the block like other people; however, she only had cats, so Voula decided to train Ginger by tying a rope round his neck and by teaching him instructions. Much to her dismay, Ginger obtusely refused to cooperate! Next, Voula decided to walk him, so she carefully explained everything to Ginger and commanded him to come with her. The cat tried to pull away as it didn't appreciate having a rope round its neck. Amazingly for Voula, her furry little friend didn't seem to want to go for a walk with her! However, she decided he would get used to it if she was just as stubborn as he, too. It became a battle of wills: she was determined the cat would obey her and not she him. Voula ended up dragging poor Ginger all the way around the block! Ginger did not oblige her at all, resisting all the way. When they got back home and Ginger was finally free, he high-tailed it out of there as fast as he could go! Voula felt so sorry for Ginger she never tried walking him ever again. She also felt guilty of a crime. She finally understood that, besides giving a cat a bath, dragging a cat around by its neck was one of the worst things you could do to a cat! After all that effort and struggle Voula learnt one thing: cats are not like dogs, so it's not a good idea to treat them as such.

 Of course Voula also had her "pet" ants to secretly feed and care for every other day or so. Besides these cares, the family acquired two budgerigars, but they escaped several weeks later by lifting up the door of their cage. First one flew out when the other lifted the cage door, then the other flew out since the door got stuck open. They were very clever really, but it had been very distressing to lose them like that. In fact it was devastating to think that the budgies didn't love them and had wanted to escape! Argyro never replaced those budgies.

 Instead the children got some tadpoles which they tried to grow into frogs. They had found them in a little stream not far from home where the water was very still and couldn't move much, because of the twigs that had formed a little dam. At school Voula had been fascinated when her grade 5 teacher, Miss Slater, had shown a film (on reels) about how tadpoles grew back legs, then front legs and then their tails fell off. Hey presto ….frogs!

 V-E-R-Y interesting indeed! So the siblings had made some

nets from Argyro's old stockings and following their mother's instructions, had tied them to long sticks and had gone looking for tadpoles. Once caught, they were put in bottles with some of the water and taken home for observation. However, a problem soon developed. What does one feed one's tadpoles? It proved difficult to solve as there was no Google back then!

Voula and Peter tried bread crumbs because they knew the ducks on the pond, at the Botanical Gardens, loved bread. Just to be sure, they threw in some grass and bird seed too, but the tadpoles didn't become frogs at all. In fact they died. Another devastating blow for the kids!

Some time later the family got a medium-sized, black, mongrel dog they named Prince (Theo only ever called him "Charlie", in honour of Prince Charles). This dog was very territorial and one day the neighbour's one-eyed dog, Cindy, a sturdy cross sausage-dog, got through a gap in the fence onto Prince's turf. Prince and Cindy growled ominously at each other and then attacked, biting each other furiously and finally locking jaws. There was a great kerfuffle as the Shmitz children, along with Peter, Jimmy and Voula called and screamed at their dogs, but to no avail. It seemed they were determined to have a duel to the death! Argyro finally heard the noise and came out, as did Mrs. Shmitz. Argyro turned the hose on the dogs, which startled them enough so that everyone was able to separate the warring parties. The hole in the fence was carefully mended and Prince and Cindy had to be content growling and barking at each other.

Next on the pet scene came Peter's pigeons. Now, Bob across the road had a lot of pigeons and Peter, being his best mate, became involved and learnt a lot about caring for them and racing them against other pigeon owners. There was a pigeon club that met monthly to release their pigeons and time them, to see whose pigeons arrived home first and second, etc. Peter told his siblings there were pigeons that specialised in *catching* or befriending other pigeons and taking them back to their coop with them. There were also racing pigeons that were fast flyers. However, all the birds would normally return home: they were "homing pigeons". When released they would fly around their coop once or twice to get their bearings. After that they would take off, flying around in the sky for an hour or so, before returning home. If they were late the boys worried, because they thought maybe someone's catcher pigeon may have tried to lead their birds to its own coop. Peter wanted pigeons, so Bob eventually gave Peter his first two pigeons to start him off, and Argyro helped Peter make a cage for them by converting the outdoor loo. They used chicken wire to make the cage. In it they built shelves and made boxes for the pigeons to build their nests in. Also, to make the birds happy, they added some perches, as well as a landing platform in front of the opening into the cage.

Before long the pigeons mated, two eggs were produced and the parents were trying to hatch them, when Peter went into the cage to inspect his prize. Soon after that the pigeons pushed their eggs out of the nest, which smashed on the concrete floor below. Bob told Peter that he shouldn't touch the eggs, as the parents smell humans and destroy their eggs out of fear. It was very sad because the little birds had already formed inside their shell houses. Next time Pete's pigeons produced their pair of eggs no one was allowed near them, until the happy day Peter burst into the kitchen to inform his mum that he had babies!

Everyone went to the cage to have a sticky beak at the juvenile pigeons. Yep, two living, chirping, featherless and pretty ugly-looking little pigeons sat in a nest. The family stayed well back to avoid another catastrophe. However, sometimes a fledgling was pecked to death by its own sibling or parent. Maybe only one was enough for the parents to handle. It seemed very harsh to Voula but nature is tough. Surviving birds eventually grew fluffy feathers, but different ones from the adult feathers of their parents.

Peter started breeding the pigeons and ended up with about twenty-five homing pigeons. He bought little numbered metal rings, from the pigeon club, and put them on their legs to identify them and Peter as their owner. In no time, Bob and Peter had a little business going on, as more eggs were hatched and baby pigeons produced. Peter's friends bought some of his pigeons as it all looked like a lot of fun.

One day Peter and Voula were told to clean the cage floor of all the bird droppings. They had to shovel the thick,

metal rings

stinky layer out, into a wheel barrow and then wheel it down and dump it out onto an unused section of the back yard. It made good fertiliser after it dried out a bit! After that, the cage was hosed out and properly cleaning.

In order to avoid any sudden deaths due to fright, the pigeons were released to fly around and the young feathered pigeons were removed and cared for by Voula as she sat on the grass in the front yard, well away from the hosing action. She protected five young fledglings in her lap. She looked at them. They were old enough to touch without the parents killing them. For some reason as the birds got a bit older the parents didn't mind if humans picked up their young. The children had accidentally discovered this fact when they picked a baby up off the floor where it had fallen, and put it back in its nest. They had waited to rescue it from murdering parents, but it had been accepted and not been pecked to death. Consequently, now Voula handled the babies without fear of hurting them as she lovingly stroked them. She touched their holey ears and twisted their necks around to see how far they could turn; it was about 270 degrees!

It got her thinking how she could help Peter with his pigeons. Out of the blue, she hit on a good idea: she could train them to be strong flyers by training them *early*! Then Peter's pigeons would become renowned for being the best and fastest racing pigeons in the region! They would be like "super pigeons" and Peter would win his races against Bob's experienced fliers. Peter would be happy about that and she would be in his good books.

While Peter was busily hosing out the cage, Voula gingerly collected them in the folds of her skirt, then carefully placed them on the grass. She knelt beside them and spoke soft, encouraging words to allay their fears. Then, one by one, she picked them up into her cupped hands and gently tossed them up a few centimetres—so far so good. They would flap their stick-like wings in an attempt to keep their balance. Voula knew that using their little immature wings would help their muscles to develop. In her mind's eye she could see the victory of a superior breed of pigeons!

She diligently persisted with each of the five fledglings. After she had exercised each bird, she started at the beginning again and repeated the process. It was important not to quit or to get bored. When she ceased from her labours, she found that the birds were looking tired and droopy. She would continue their exercises tomorrow. "Too much exercise," thought Voula. "Next time I should go slower." To her dismay, the birds drooped even more and finally, one after the other, stopped breathing! The ground came up to meet her! With shock and terror she realised Peter's surprise would be one of sadness, horror and anger; not pleasant at all. What would he do?

    Maybe she wouldn't tell him about her pigeon exercise classes so he wouldn't know she was the one responsible for their untimely deaths! If he didn't know, he wouldn't be upset with her. However, Voula felt so guilty, she had to confess the truth to him and so she told him she had been trying to help him, to have the best pigeons ever, and took him to the grass where she had left the deceased birds. When Peter looked upon the corpses, he was very upset and Voula explained she had tried to strengthen them, but it had all back-fired! Peter was certainly not happy, but there was no bellicosity and he did not hit her, but he did something worse: he told her to keep away from his pigeons. Anyhow, that lasted a few weeks and then he forgave her. After all, he appreciated the help Voula could give him with shovelling the droppings and keeping the cage clean.

    The next time she got involved with the pigeons was to come to Peter's rescue. One morning, when Voula was inspecting a litter of kittens, in the outside laundry, near the pigeon cage, Peter came running in, white-faced, "My Catcher is stuck in some wire and she's bleeding. I can't get her down. Do something Voula!" They went to inspect the situation together. About a metre above their heads, was Peter's prized pigeon, a "catcher" that lured other pigeons into the coop. The bird's foot, just above its claw, was pierced through with some cage wire; it had pierced right through the pigeon's leg, so that it could not move. It was held fast, even though it had struggled a little to get away from

Voula as she approached the injured bird. Peter got a pair of pliers but couldn't stomach the task ahead of him. "Come on Voula. You can do it–you're tough." Voula knew this was her big chance to redeem herself and to impress her resourceful, younger brother. It was the perfect opportunity to help him! Voula felt she should not fear failure, but rather fear not trying! She took the pliers from Peter, climbed up the cage a bit, gritted her teeth and cut the wire.

Peter took the bird. "Do you think it's going to live?" he asked uncertainly: this was his pitiful prized catcher. Voula tried to sound confident, "Yeah, she'll be alright." Together with Peter they held the bird and prepared a bath of water mixed with pink Condy's crystals to disinfect the leg.

Over the next few days, the kids watched the bird as it flew about in the cage. The other birds didn't want it near them. It was a great relief when the foot healed, but it remained swollen and the bird hopped when it walked on the ground. Peter was very grateful to Voula for her help, and even went so far as to express his own inadequacy in aiding the injured pigeon. He told Voula she had saved the pigeon's life! That was music to Voula's ears as Peter did not often give her praise. It didn't matter that the bird's leg was unusable, because it was alive, and Voula had earned Peter's respect. "This is the beginning of a new relationship!" thought Voula. Little did she realise what the future held!

the pidgeon with the permanently damaged leg

When Peter and Voula were 8 and 9, people often mistook them for twins.

Jimmy with Peter's fledgling pigeons, and below with an adult one.

Chapter 21
The Billy-Cart

It was Saturday morning and Voula was looking for something to do. From inside the house, she could hear the banging sounds of a hammer. Out of curiosity, she followed the noise out into the back yard. The banging was coming from the old garage. The wooden door of the garage had fallen off and had been left leaning on the side wall of the garage, until Theo had enough time to fix it, so it was easy for her to look inside. What did she see? Peter and his friend Bob Tydon, from across the road, were busily nailing together bits of wood—long pieces of timber and shorter ones too. They also had four wheels, about 20 cm in diameter, waiting on the old table they were working on. It looked very interesting. Voula hoped that maybe they would let her be part of their latest project!

"Whatsha doin' boys?" she asked. "Makin' a billy-cart!" was Bob's short reply. "Ooh, can I help too?" inquired Voula hopefully. "Nah! This is boy stuff!" Disappointed, Voula left them to their business. They were banging and nailing all afternoon.

When they finally emerged from the garage, they were pulling a sturdy-looking billy-cart behind them. It looked pretty plain and simple, but it's the construction of the foundation that stands the test of time! "Who's going down the Hill first?" asked Peter hopeful of the honour of being the first. "I will," answered Bob, "but only if you want me to." "OK!" conceded Peter. Bob and Peter agreed on everything. Peter had great respect for Bob who was a couple of years older!

Their houses were in Byron Street, named after the famous English poet and lover of Greek art. Argyro had told her children about Lord Byron and they thought it was quite a privilege to live in a street bearing his name. Happily for Peter and Bob, Byron Street also had a famous neighbourhood hill, Billy Goat Hill, just outside their front gates. Some people think the hill was named because of some goats kept on an empty block behind Bob's house. Billy Goat Hill in Byron Street is only a hill, not a big mountain, but to the kids in the neighbourhood it was big enough!

Peter and his mate, Bob, parked the billy-cart on top of the hill. They knew the road rules so they kept it on the left side of the road. Unfortunately, the boys had a small problem: their billy-cart didn't have any brakes! How would they stop the billy-cart? Well they would use their shoes and Bob have a pair of trusty R.M. Williams boots! By dragging them along the road he hoped to slow down and eventually stop their billy-cart. Peter, the inventor, advised his friend, "Bob, just stop by putting your feet down on the road." Bob looked a bit scared but he was a brave boy. He wanted to vindicate Peter's trust in him, to take the maiden drive on their billy-cart and to prove that their billy-cart was a good one. Nothing would stop him going down that hill!

Well, it was reckoned about twelve kids gathered round the billy-cart that day, to watch it go down Billy Goat Hill on its inaugural drive! It was very exciting for everyone. Gathered around the cart were: Bob's big sister, the three Shmitz kids from next-door, a couple of boys from down the road, Voula, Jimmy and the four Hadis children. Maybe there were one or two others but it's hard to say. It was a memorable day! All the kids appreciated the special privilege of "driving" on the road. It was a big step, being in a "vehicle" like an adult!

Where were the parents you might ask? In those days kids were often left to themselves and most of the time they had no idea what their kids were up to. As long as they were around the neighbourhood, it was okay. "Quality time" for parents and kids had not been thought of yet: parents worked while children played together.

Some of the kids were jealous of the billy-cart and told Bob it wouldn't work properly. However, they waited to see what would happen, in case the billy-cart actually did perform. If it did, then some of them wanted to drive the billy-cart too! You must understand that Hamilton is a country town. There is not very much traffic in residential streets; especially on weekends when all the shops close at noon on Saturday. In those days no one worked, or played sport, on Sundays. Therefore, it was a fair bet that no cars would interfere with Bob's ride down Billy Goat Hill.

Holding the rope tightly in his hands, Bob tested the cart. When he pulled the rope with his left hand, the front wheels indeed turned left. When he tugged it with his right hand, the wheels turned to the right. Next he checked the brakes: he was wearing his tough leather boots. He was ready! Peter started the countdown as Bob sat grimly on the billy-cart, staring straight ahead, "10, 9, 8, 7, 6,…." All the other kids joined in, "….5, 4, 3, 2, 1 TAKE OFF!"

Bob was off! He pushed with his boots. The cart was slow at first but quickly picked-up speed as it went down the crest of Billy Goat Hill. Now he was flying! There was no way Bob could stop even if he wanted to, because he was going too fast!

At the bottom of the hill was the intersection of Byron and Goldsmith Streets. As fate would have it, just as Bob approached the intersection, Voula could see another vehicle on Goldsmith Street heading towards the bottom of Billy Goat Hill. Poor Bob might be killed! Bob saw the car and he must have felt his death was near! What could he do? The onlookers held their breaths and watched, mesmerised as the saga unfolded. Quickly pulling with his left hand Bob tugged at the rope and stuck his right foot out the side of the cart for balance. As he turned sharply to the left into Goldsmith Street, the car *just* missed him and the driver yelled out something at him! Bob breathed again with relief. He was still alive! All the kids cheered. Bob had done it and was their new hero! However, from then on, they had a new system. Someone waited at the bottom of Billy Goat Hill and gave a signal when there were no cars coming. Then the billy-cart could take-off safely: unless a speeding car came along unexpectedly.

All the boys eagerly lined up for turns going down Billy Goat Hill. However, after what Voula had just witnessed, with how fast Bob went down the Hill and his near-death experience, she was too scared to use the cart. Regardless, she felt she should save face and ask for a turn too. Anyway, the boys made it easy for her. "No girls allowed!" they decided. Voula was secretly thankful but pretended to be offended, "That's not fair!" she snapped, and stomped away.

Secretly, she hoped one day she too would have the courage of her little brother, to go down Billy Goat Hill…but not today. Maybe another time. "The boys really are very brave," she meditated to herself. Voula didn't know what the future held for her…she *would* get a go on the billy-cart, but *not* to go down Billy Goat Hill!

Out the back was the outdoor laundry. On the left side is the new washing machine with its hand rotated wringers (beside a copper water-boiler).

On the right is the garage with its broken door leaning on the wall and inside can be seen the old table where the boys built their billy-cart.

Argyro and Peter walking up Billy Goat Hill.

looking at the two church steeples from the top of Billy Goat Hill (circa 1928-1954)

Chapter 22
The Monorail

Voula could see that the boys always had a lot of fun going down Billy Goat Hill in the billy-cart, so finally, one day, she summoned up enough courage to ask for a ride. "No way! No girls allowed!" Peter and Bob chorused as usual. After a few weeks of much use, the billy-cart's wheels were bent and twisted. This was because the boys were rough and often crashed the billy-cart, on purpose. Anyway, the day arrived when the cart wouldn't move any more. It was busted!

Once again, hammering was heard from the garage as Peter nailed a "backrest" on the cart, because he wanted to improve it and make it more comfortable. He tried to fix the wheels but they were too twisted. Not to worry: Peter had a plan!

The week before, Peter had seen a monorail train on the telly on the Disneyland show televised from the USA. It was part of *Tomorrow Land* and took people around the park to view the sights. Peter had been fascinated by the monorail, so he decided to make one. Guess what he was going to use?

Peter set to work. He found an old pulley in the garage. It was a rusty pulley about 4cm in diameter, but how could he use it to make a monorail cart? Well he would find a way; after all necessity is the mother of invention! All day he thought and thought until he hit on an idea.

Peter got some rope and tied the front and back ends of the cart in a big loop. Then he connected a second rope through the pulley and the rope holding the cart. He dragged the cart along the yard to the back fence where there was a tall plum tree about six or seven metres high. He left the cart at the base of the tree and picked up a long piece of rope.

Carefully climbing the tree, Peter quickly reached the top and tied one end of the rope to a sturdy branch. Then he climbed back down and went in search of Bob and Jimmy. He would need help: the more hands the better. (For your information, Peter grew up to become a civil engineer.)

By the time he got back with his two helpers Voula had also turned up. "Whatsha doin' boys?" she asked hopefully. "Making a monorail," answered Peter in a matter-of-fact way. He had climbed onto the bottom branch and while the others were lifting the cart, Peter was pulling it up with the rope. Voula helped to lift it too, as the boys didn't mind that. Well, they were at it all afternoon. Sometimes the cart slipped down and they had to start all over again. It was a great struggle, but at last the cart was hanging along the rope and connected to the pulley, hovering about three metres above the ground! They all admired their handiwork. It looked spectacular up there!

Peter then got the other end of the rope and tied it carefully to a thick post on the side fence. The monorail could now, theoretically, slide down along the rope on the pulley, from the tree top to the fence. It was an engineering success and ready to go! Now someone had to test it to see if it would really work, but who? Jimmy was the smallest and the lightest but he refused. It looked too dangerous for him: he was a smart boy!

"Voula if you want to, you can have a turn on the monorail," Peter offered kindly. Voula knew he needed a guinea pig, but at the same time she felt honoured to be asked because it was not often that she was invited to "play with the boys". She had recently climbed to the top of that plum tree and wasn't as afraid of heights as she normally was. She had always been a chicken when it came to high places: they made her legs feel like jelly! "Okay then, I'll do it!" Voula agreed.

The boys watched as she carefully climbed up to the top branch where the cart was hanging. Then she hesitated. The monorail didn't look very strong. "Just get in!" Peter advised her. "How?" she asked him. "It swings away when I try to get in."

Peter instructed her, "Put one foot in and then quickly lean in and sit on the seat." Voula really wanted to get this right so she reached out with her foot and steadied the monorail. Then as quick as lightning, she sort of made herself fall into the seat! However, she didn't have long to enjoy her privileged position. In a moment she felt herself and the cart falling!

"Aarhhh!" Voula let out a short-lived atavistic cry of dread. The next thing she knew, she was sitting in the cart on the ground. The *monorail* had not slid along the rope at all! It had come straight down! Fear gripped her as she realised there was a strange, tingling sensation along her spine where the timber backrest had scraped along her back. Now Voula was afraid to move. "I think I might be paralysed," she spoke huskily to her brothers. Voula had just finished reading a novel, "What Katy Did", by Susan Coolidge, about an American tomboy who got paralysed after falling off a high-flying swing, so paralysis had come immediately into her mind.

"Don't be stupid!" Peter responded and to her incredulity, the boys dashed off to play together, leaving her on the ground. Voula had half-expected some sympathy but now she felt angry and frustrated. "Don't they care about me?" she pondered to herself. Tears stung her eyes. Her back was hurting and it was still tingling. She decided that the best thing to do was to lie still for a while, perhaps until night time! Maybe her mother would miss her and come and help her. She was feeling sorry for herself.

After a while, she felt bored of waiting. By now, her back had stopped tingling, so Voula tried to move her legs. To her great relief, they functioned! She wasn't paralysed after all! Slowly, carefully, she got up. She felt very lucky for she had thought she would be crippled and in a wheelchair, just like Katy in the novel!

Chapter 23
Sticks and Stones

Voula was lucky because at school the girls had their own designated playground apart from the boys, who were quite rough as they tackled each other in their ball games. Jimmy was too young to play with the big boys and was quite happy in a playground with friends from his kinder years, but Peter was not so lucky. Being a feisty boy, he enjoyed physical activity and was often on the footy ground at school. Pete enjoyed football and the contact of pushing and shoving did not bother him. It was normal for him to come home with scratches, scrapes and bruises.

One day, while Argyro was working at the cafe as a waitress during the lunchtime rush, she had an unexpected visit from Pete's teacher. Since the school was only about 250 metres away, it was not problematical. However, the teacher raised Argyro's eyebrows by telling her that Pete was daily involved in playground fighting! Worse, the teacher believed Peter was the instigator of the fights. She requested Argyro put a stop to Peter's belligerence towards the other boys. Argyro was shocked because this information had come out of nowhere, and she knew her son did not have a mean bone in his body. Pete himself had not complained about the boys at school. Her response, the very next day, was to go to the playground to see for herself what was going on during lunchtime.

The racket of school children during playtime is familiar to all of us, but nothing prepared Argyro for what she saw. There on top of some playground equipment was Peter, with Steven Hadis and some other "wogs" beside him. They were defending themselves against a ring of Anglo-Celtic boys who were yelling abuse at them. Peter was brandishing a long stick and fighting off his attackers. He was teasing them with a little chorus, "Sticks and stones will break my bones but names will never hurt me!"

Argyro could see her son was protecting himself and felt proud that he was brave enough to stand up for himself. Peter and his friends were greatly outnumbered, but they did not seem too distressed, rather they appeared to enjoy the challenge and treated it as a fighting game. After all, the best form of defence is offence, and if anyone could complain of bad behaviour it should be Argyro, because Peter was simply defending himself. She told the school headmaster she felt Peter should be allowed to defend himself and she complained that her son was being bullied. The school criticisms ceased and she never mentioned it to Peter until many, many years later when he was an adult.

It seems being a "wog" in Hamilton posed a few problems and Voula and Peter found themselves on the receiving end of some bullying out of school hours too. As they were walking home from school they were attacked by acorn missiles aimed at their heads, chests and legs. It really hurt, but all they could do was to use their arms to cover their faces and "run for it". They hoped it was a one-off, but the attacks continued and even intensified as other boys joined in the "fun." It appeared that the playground fighting had spilled out onto the streets! Now it was difficult for Jimmy, Voula and Peter to get to and from school, because little groups of boys waited in ambush along the way. It became a "war game" as piles of acorns were collected and used as ammunition against them. Peter always fought back with his own acorns, but Voula and Jimmy would run away. Even Bob Tydon became involved because he was often in Pete's company, as they played around the neighbourhood.

Bob and Pete didn't want to appear weak so they went on the offensive. After school, they would go down Billy Goat Hill to the oak trees in the park beside the pool, carrying bags they wanted to cram with acorns for ammunition. When they were prepared, they went looking for their "enemies" and started "shooting" their acorns at the other boys. They took cover behind trees and fences as their adversaries, who seemed to enjoy it, fought back.

Because neither Argyro nor Theo had a driver's licence, their children, like most children in those days, walked to school, about 650 meters away from home. However, it was fast getting out of hand as walking to and from school became a real problem. Therefore, it was a great relief to the kids when Argyro shared this issue with Theo, who decided to hire a taxi to deliver his kids to and from school every weekday. This went on for about half a year and meanwhile Peter was forbidden to go out and look for acorns! After that, life returned to normal, and walking to school resumed again.

Racism appears to have been ubiquitous in the 1960s and even adults suffered trouble. When Argyro was at home and Jimmy was yet a baby, she heard some stones hitting her windows and roof. The next day was the same, so she took note of the time and waited the following day to see what would eventuate. Sure enough two boys, on their way home from school, took aim at her house and threw stones they had collected for that purpose. They were aged ten years or thereabouts. Next day Argyro stood outside in her front yard when the boys swaggered past. To her infinite surprise they took aim and threw stones at *her* and one even hit her *baby*! They quickly ran down the road, but Argyro decided to take action and followed the boys at a distance to see where they lived, with the aim of talking to their parents. They had slowed down because they had not realised Argyro was following them. When they reached the park beside the swimming pool, at the bottom of Billy Goat Hill, they suddenly noticed her and started running.

Argyro gently placed Jimmy on the grass and pursued the boys. As she got closer she threatened them and screamed at them never to come near her house again. They kept running and didn't look back, but she never had any trouble with stone throwing again. In fact, one day as Argyro was walking along her street she saw a lady approaching. The lady was looking flabbergasted with the behaviour of her son, who was trying to hide himself from view, by using his mother as a shield. As the lady and Argyro passed one another, Argyro saw the boy was one of her former antagonists, who was now red-faced and very subdued! His mother did not know what to make of it and Argyro smiled to herself.

the entrance to the pool

the park beside the swimming pool

at the Hamilton Baths (circa summer 1962-63)

from left to right: John Hadis, Argyro's sister visiting from Melbourne, Peggy Hadis, Peter, Jimmy, Voula, Theo Hadis, Argyro's nephew Theo, and Argyro

the swimming pool plaque showing it opened in 1955

Chapter 24
The Pipe Tunnel and Prince

Standing in the park next to Hamilton's swimming pool, Voula couldn't believe her eyes! She stared into the dark opening in front of her. Peter, his mate Bob and Steven Hadis had gone into the huge pipe tunnel from where a steady stream of water poured out. The pipes were about two metres wide and about the same height. Since the pipe tunnel wasn't finished, it had been left open, and the stream left to escape and meander along its pebble bed. Actually it took another couple of years before it was completed and covered up. However, to a child, a couple of years is a lifetime! Until the work was finished the children enjoyed playing there while their parents were completely oblivious of the fact!

Now Voula watched the water as it gurgled out of the open pipe and continued on its way, to eventually join the Glenelg River. The adventurous boys had said they wanted to go "exploring". For goodness sake! Didn't they realise how dangerous it was to go in there?

After a few minutes she could hear them shouting somewhere in the pipe tunnel and enjoying the echo of their voices. Voula slowly walked into the mouth of the tunnel and made some noises to hear the effect. This was fun! Maybe she could go in further. As she walked there was a sudden turn and everything became pitch black. She stretched out her hand, but she couldn't even see it! This was too much for her to handle and she turned around and ran outside into the daylight. However, she didn't want to be scared of the dark while her younger brother proved so intrepid. She tried entering the tunnel again and this time she picked up the family dog, Prince, for comfort and carried him into the tunnel for company. Still, because she couldn't see where she was walking, it really frightened her. Prince wasn't much help either, because he was whining and wriggling to get free: he didn't like it either. What if he could smell some danger? What if a stranger was hiding in here; or maybe a poisonous eel or a snake? She had seen eels in the stream, so she knew they could easily be in the tunnel too. Her fear got the better of her and she turned back. The boys' voices had vanished and she wondered where they were. Voula had a passing thought: would they get out unhurt? How would she explain all of this to her mother?

After about half an hour Steven came running towards her. To her surprise he was carefully traversing along the tops of the pipes above the ground and not through the pipe tunnel! "How did you get out?" Voula queried. Steven explained, "There's an opening near Thompson Street outside the footy oval." Voula was still worried and asked, "Where are the others?" Steven responded that they were returning in the tunnel, but that he was too scared to follow suit. Even though they called him a *chicken*, he still didn't want to return through the tunnel! Voula could understand exactly how he felt. She could relate to Steven's common sense and honest frankness. Not everyone is a rash super hero! It was amazing because to get to the other end, the boys had travelled about one and a half kilometres *inside* the tunnel in darkness. Voula thought they were crazy!

It soon became a favourite place for the boys who often went into those pipes to play. Once the boys had a close shave: a water snake had slithered along inside the tunnel and had given them a good scare! Well as we know, danger begets caution, so the boys made a decision for their safety: they would ride their bikes in the tunnel, just in case another snake came along! Inconveniently, when they did ride their bikes, they couldn't climb out at the other end of the tunnel, because the Thompson Street opening had a partial grate which they could climb through, but it was too small for their bikes. Therefore, they always had to hang a U-turn and come back to the mouth of the tunnel next to the swimming pool.

Sometimes Voula and Prince would go running along the stream to where it joined the Grange Burn River. A little further along, there was a bridge with no name, on Portland Road, just before it becomes the Henty Highway. Under the bridge, it was shady and secretive where Voula enjoyed the gentle sounds of running water and the croaking of the frogs in the water reeds. It was a favourite spot for Voula and Prince, and also for the other kids.

One day the Hadis brothers, Peter and Bob rode their bikes to the bridge. They saw Peggy Hadis and Voula with Prince sitting below the bridge. The girls' bikes were lying on the grass beside them as they talked and listened to the quiet sounds around them. They were pulling at the long green grass beside them. After a few minutes Peter called Prince to come to him. The dog ran up the slope and wagged his tail against Peter's leg. What did Prince look like? He was a black mongrel about fifty centimetres high. He was a good dog, but he didn't like water and he hated having a bath! Prince didn't know what Pete had decided to do! Peter wanted his dog to learn to swim, and there was only one way Peter knew how to do that: he picked up his unsuspecting pet and dropped him over the bridge into the river, three metres below!

Peggy and Voula stared in horror as Prince helplessly flailed his legs before he dropped into the water! Bubbles came up where Prince had plummeted into the river. It had been a belly wacker fall so it must have hurt poor Princey! The children waited for him to emerge, but only more bubbles emerged to the water's surface. Everyone felt badly for Prince, even Peter had his doubts! Voula called his name repeatedly, hoping he could hold his breath under water for what seemed like an eternity.

Just when everyone thought Prince had breathed his last, he suddenly popped his head out of the water. The girls called to him as he swam clumsily to the water's edge. However, he didn't stop alongside them for some comforting hugs. Prince ran up the slope and raced away from the children. He had experienced a horrible fright and maybe he thought the kids had tried to murder him!

From then on, his personality underwent a change and he was never the same again, as Prince became rougher and more aggressive! Whenever a car drove by the house, Prince would jump the one meter fence and chase after it. Then he would bite a back tyre and not let go until the wheel had flipped him round and round two or three times. After that he would release his grip and fall on the road, barking loudly at the receding vehicle.

He also barked at *people* walking past the house and most times he would jump the fence and attack their shoes and ankles. Whenever this happened the children tried to stop him, but unfortunately someone complained to the Dog Pound and the Dog Catcher turned up on their doorstep. He wore a Akubra hat and held a dangerous looking rifle over his shoulder. He knocked on the door loudly and the scared kids saw him framed against the daylight in the doorway and ran for their mother.

Argyro was shocked to see a stranger with a weapon at her front door, so when he demanded the dog, she shouted at him, "Get out! Get off my property!" After some arguing he left, but warned he would return to shoot the dog if he had any more complaints from the public. Alas, about four years later, Prince finally did meet an untimely death, but not at the hands of the Dog Catcher! He had escaped the back yard to chase after another dog, when he had run across Bell Street, a busy road in Melbourne, and got hit by a car. He managed to crawl back onto the footpath where Voula and Argyro, having chased after him, were helpless to do anything to save him. He died while Voula spoke his name with a trembling, fearful voice and patted him. Poor Prince! He had lived a short but exciting life!

the bridge with no name on Portland Road

Chapter 25
The Bike

Holding on to the picket fence with her left hand, Voula sat gingerly on Peter's bike trying to find her balance. She was struggling to learn how to ride a bike, but as her parents had promised her a new bicycle if she could learn to ride, she was persevering. She had managed to sort-of-ride by gripping the right handle bar with her right hand, while pushing off and trying to pedal a bit. Then she would quickly grab onto the front fences of the neighbouring houses, as she slowly rolled a small way along and fell leftwards onto the picket fences. At the moment she was leaning against Mrs. Mannings' fence, about a hundred metres from her house, but it had taken her about half an hour to get there!

Voula wished she could already ride! She wondered why her younger brother, Pete, could ride and not she? Let's face it, Peter had put in many hours of practice and now he could ride without even holding on to the handle bars! He was such a show-off! Also he could ride fast ... down Billy Goat Hill! Voula was proud of him, but she REALLY wanted to be able to ride too.

Voula painstakingly continued her efforts all the way to the corner and then had to turn left in order to continue around the block. However, she now faced two problems: there was a downhill slope and there were prickly branches poking out of a low wire fence. This would not do as she had nothing to hang on to, while she tried to steer the bike and pedal simultaneously. Voula had a challenge because if she turned around to ride back, then she would have to hold the handle bar with her left hand and grab onto the fences with her right one. She was right-handed and so her weaker left hand would have to steer. Oh well, it was better than continuing on down a slope. The other option, of going across the road didn't work either because several fences were not high enough to hold onto.

By the time Voula got back to her house, her knuckles had been squashed against the fences several times, as had her legs. She was a mass off bruises but she felt that she had improved her riding skills a lot! She could stay balanced long enough to turn the pedals a couple of times and had rolled past a couple of houses without holding onto their fences.

A few weeks later she was riding Peter's bike quite well, but unluckily had bent the handle of Peter's bike bell against a fence. Peter didn't like his bike getting wrecked by his big sister, but it was a sign of things to come. (She totalled his "souped up" Holden when she was twenty-one, but he forgave her!) Both Pete and Voula were happy when Argyro and Theo bought Voula a new bike for her eleventh birthday. It was pink and later on had a white basket attached to the front handlebars. Voula could eventually ride very well, even without holding the handles, just like her younger brother: but not *fast* down Billy Goat Hill. Commonly, in those days bikes didn't have gears and it was easy to brake by pushing backwards on the pedals: very instinctive and easy to understand and use. Voula and Peter used to keep their bikes in the back yard, leaning against the broken garage door.

One particular day, Voula and Peter had a dispute and as she walked into the back yard she saw Peter's bike, with its bent bell, resting in its usual place. It was then she thought of a shady plan to get even with him. She furtively let down one of his bike tyres. Later, Peter headed for his bike as he planned going for a ride to the local milk bar to get some footie cards (they came inside bubble gum packets). No surprises that being an accomplished prankster himself, he soon added up one and one and confronted Voula with her misdeed, to which she soon glibly confessed; she could never keep a straight face whilst lying.

Soon Voula saw the tell-tale signs of rage building up in Peter: his face was changing colour from pink to dark red to almost purple! She backed away, but Peter was incensed and took his revenge by kicking and bending the spokes of Voula's new bike. She told on him, to their long suffering mother, but Argyro didn't want to get involved in their squabble. Voula pretended she didn't care and left her bike unattended for a few days. Then she went out and straightened the wheel spokes as best as she could. She washed her bike and shone it up, but it was no longer *perfect*. She should not have wronged Peter and now she was suffering the consequences. It was a good lesson to learn: don't plan evil and do bad things to others because it'll all come back to bite you!

A few of the neighbourhood kids had bikes and so did one or two of the Hadis children. Hence, they used to go riding out of the town and into the local paddocks. Voula helpfully put Prince in her basket so she could give him a lift, until his paws got sore gripping onto the wire and he wriggled, causing the handle bars to swivel and Voula to crash. Sometimes Voula used to dink Peggy on her bike, until she too got her own one. In this way the kids explored interesting, scenic spots and sometimes went "mushrooming". It was also fun to jump on toadstools and mushrooms and squash them into the ground. Why is that?

Another time the troupe of kids, some on bikes and some on foot, came across an old wooden bridge with a railway track going over it. While the kids had a rest and a bit of a picnic in the grass below the bridge, Peter, Bob Tydon and Steven Hadis decided to walk across the bridge. Isn't that what it was there for? Sure, it takes courage to test your limits and to try new things, but it takes wisdom to accept your limits. The trouble was that the boys didn't have much wisdom! They were gallivanting and happily frolicking and egging each other on, as they jumped across the beams of the bridge, when they suddenly froze with dread. First they heard and then they saw a train coming straight towards them! What could they do? They had earlier noticed that every now and then, there were some enclosed overhangs on the bridge, for just such an occasion. The boys quickly scampered to safety as the train hurtled past them. "That was close," the boys thought to themselves. "How do we always get ourselves into sticky situations?" They put on brave faces when they returned to the others!

Sometimes, as Voula rode along the country roads in the sunshine, she would look into the distance and think she could see a shimmer of water across the road. Bob told her it was a mirage! Sure enough as they got closer to the "water", it disappeared and yet another watery pond appeared across the road on the horizon.

Those long, summery days seemed endless to the children and they packed a lot into one day. They wished their adventures would never end as they each loved the companionship of the other kids and the beauty of their natural surroundings. Sadly, with every majestically coloured sky, at sunset they had to "go in". Goodbyes were said to companions with a twinge of sadness, that such a glorious day could ever end, and it was time to go to sleep!

Chapter 26
The Bicycle Lesson

Voula's confidence riding her bike grew to the point she felt able to teach Steven Hadis how to ride his bike! (Actually it was Peggy's bike but Peggy allowed her brother to ride it because he didn't have one of his own.) Steven was considered a bit of a chicken by the boys he played with, because he didn't mind admitting when he was scared, and wouldn't do something he felt unable to do. It was humiliating for Steven that he couldn't ride a bike, because even his sister, Peggy could ride one! Anyhow, when all the kids wanted to go for a picnic or go exploring on their bikes, Steven had to either be dinked or just jog along, so it made things a bit difficult. Therefore, finally one day, he built up his courage and admitted to Voula that he wanted to learn to ride, like the rest of them. She immediately offered to help him as she felt sorry for him, and as he was nearly two years younger than she, her maternal instincts took over!

First she instructed him to sit on the seat and try to balance himself, while she held the bike and rolled it down the gentle slope on the side of her house. Steven wobbled the bike terribly and it took a lot of patience on Voula's part not to give up. Steven declared he was hopeless, which made Voula even more determined than ever to help this guy! So she kept encouraging him and telling him that he could do it if he didn't give up. They kept rolling down the little incline and walking up to start again.

Up, down, up down. At last Steven decided he had got the hang of it! He was certainly starting to enjoy himself! He could ride after all. Steven thanked Voula repeatedly, giving her full credit for his success. Steven was really quite a humble little fellow…. well not that little, because he was a bit chubby. Her felt gratified!

Since they were on a roll, so to speak, Voula wanted to continue her help, although Steven felt he had achieved enough for one day and gave the excuse of feeling tired. However, Voula was eager and persuaded Steven to try riding down Billy Goat Hill. She smilingly told him, "If you can do this, you can ride anywhere. There will be no need for *any* more training. You can do it, I'm sure!" And looking into her eyes, he believed her.

With anticipation they wheeled the bike out of the front gate and over to the left side of the Hill in obedience with the road rules. Sadly, Steven's courage evaporated like fog on a sunny day, as the gradient of the Hill overawed him. "I can't do this! It's too hard; maybe another day." Steven's voice betrayed his fear, although he half regretted his outburst, because he really wished he *could* ride down the Hill. Perhaps he secretly wanted Voula to insist, so that if he failed, he could blame Voula's bossiness. Whatever Steven's thoughts, Voula felt she could see the opportunity, to sure success, slipping away. "No, no you'll be okay. Trust me!" she begged. Her confidence was infectious and Steven decided she must be right. He braced himself. "I'll do it," he announced to an enraptured Voula. She proposed, "I'll hold onto the back of your seat so you don't fall. Don't worry." Steven felt relieved to hear it.

To add to their moment of glory, Peter, Jimmy and the other Hadis children were coming up the Hill, when they spied Steven about to do what he had never done before! "What a moment!"

thought Voula, "Steven will be so happy." She imagined it all in her mind's eye, Steven riding along, laughing with the other boys as they went riding into the countryside, exploring unknown regions. It would be great and she would get some credit too! She felt her pride swell up as her heart nearly broke with its full quota of joy.

"Go Steve!" she cajoled him, holding onto his seat. But Steve reneged! "No. I'll fall. I…I'm not ready for Billy Goat Hill yet!" stammered poor Steve. Now Voula had put herself in an invidious position, but risked it. She didn't give up and stubbornly badgered Steve, until he pushed off with his legs and got his balance on the bike, as Voula grabbed onto his bike saddle. He rolled down the slope quite nicely and the other kids walking up started cheering him.

About one-third of the way down Billy Goat Hill, Steven picked up speed and Voula's grip on the seat was no more, because she couldn't keep up. So now Steven was on his own and fear was in his eyes. If it wasn't for the gravel on the side of the road, Steve might have made it all the way down Billy Goat Hill, but as it was, he didn't have a chance! The gravel made him wobble a bit and get a little off balance, which scared him and made him wobble even more. The bike seemed to have a mind of its own! Voula saw it unfold in slow motion. The bicycle wobbled so much that Steven lost control of it. He only made it to about the two-third mark down the Hill, when he hit the gravel on the road. Steven let out a scream of terror but no one could save him. He fell hard and Voula held her breath. Had he broken his teeth…his neck? Recall that people didn't wear bicycle helmets.

Steven got up shakily on his feet as Voula rushed to help

him. He had scratches on his face, hands and legs which were bleeding. "Get away from me! This is all your fault!" screamed Steven. Voula was humiliated and distressed by Steve's attitude. They had spent a lovely, friendly afternoon together, as she helped him to ride and now this was her thanks! "I shouldn't have insisted he could ride down this stupid hill, and then everything would've been fine," Voula upbraided herself in a dolorous voice. "I've stuffed-up again!" It seemed she couldn't do anything right and she shouldn't be so bossy!

All the kids agreed with the bleeding victim that it was clearly all Voula's fault. Even Peggy thought Voula had been too pushy on her younger brother, and she didn't want to talk to Voula or play with her for some time to come!

Chapter 27
The Childhood Home

What was Voula's, Peter's and Jimmy's house like? There is an old Australian dream or tradition, that every family can own their own home, with plenty of room for a Hills Hoist on their own quarter acre block, that's about 1000 m^2 of land. This was true in Hamilton and is still the case even today, according to the expression, "A man's home is his castle". Nowadays of course, most residential city blocks are about 650m^2 or smaller and our politicians are telling us to trim down our dreams and not to be selfish by spreading out and increasing the sizes of our cities. They want us to build upwards and not outwards, as former Prime Minister and Federal Treasurer, Paul Keating once famously stated when discussing housing choices in Australia. He blamed Australia's economic woes on the desire for a backyard and a Hills Hoist! Still, in country areas, the problem of urban sprawl is non-existent.

Their house in Byron Street was an old three-bedroom, weatherboard place, with a corrugated red, tin roof and then aged about sixty years old. The plaster on the walls was brittle and was cracking in places. Each room was painted a different pastel colour: the boys' bedroom was pale blue and Voula's was pink. In the kitchen were two huge storage bins that pulled out at the top, pivoting at their base and were originally built to store grain. Argyro kept her flour in one and her lentils in another.

These types of storage bins are usually only found on outback properties and in the kitchens of places like *Werribee House*, as people of a hundred years ago couldn't get fresh food supplies every day like we do these days.

Further, when Argyro and Theo first rented in Hamilton, the refrigerators had no freezer, so ice was delivered every day and put in big metal boxes to keep meat frozen. Milk and bread were also delivered daily and money was left on the front porch for the delivery man. No one stole the money, so if the money was not there, in the empty milk bottle, then the milk-man assumed the householder did not want any milk that day and he checked again the next day. If one were leaving for a holiday one left a note for the "milko" in an empty bottle, informing him when they'd return and require fresh milk. The milkman had a horse and cart with big milk canisters and milk bottles in crates. He would run to each front door with a basket crate of bottles, collect the money, pick up the empty bottles and leave the required number of full milk bottles. Bottles were always glass and the milk came only in full-cream: not low-fat or calcium enriched. Then he would run to the next house as the horse slowly plodded along the road without stopping. They made a great team and worked well together! If the horse was too far ahead the milko would whistle him to stop.

The house itself sat in the middle of the block towards the front boundary, so there was easy access to both sides of the house. As you stood facing the front of the house, there was a veranda with a camellia tree on the left side of the front yard and a massive palm tree on the right side of the garden that shaded the parental bedroom.

After much discussion, Theo and Argyro reached a decision

to cut down the palm tree because it made their room too dark and Argyro wanted more sunshine in their garden for her flowers. When a huge truck arrived, the children were ordered indoors and out of danger. They watched from their parents' bedroom as some men unloaded a large circular saw. As the saw bit into the trunk of the palm, it made a piercing scream, so the kids covered their ears, but it availed nothing as they could still hear all the racket! Finally the palm descended, but unfortunately it was so tall it landed on the camellia tree and broke some of its branches off. Argyro actually cried to see the broken branches with their beautiful pale, pink flowers, lying bruised on the ground. When Theo endeavoured to lift some of the branches he felt a sudden, sharp pain in his back. His back injuries were to plague him for the remainder of his life. After that, Theo always advised his offspring to take care of their backs, saying when one's back was hurt it was like glass with a crack in it: fragile, weak and never the same again.

In the garden, all around the fences, Argyro had planted flowers, mainly roses. To complete the picture, a cracked curved concrete path led from the front wire gate to the veranda. That was where Voula tried to learn to roller skate. The four-wheeled skates had to be attached and adjusted to her shoes. They never really fitted properly, so it was difficult to learn how to skate. She could stand on her toes and go forwards on one leg but the cracks in the path made her skating jerky and difficult to balance, especially on one leg. She never learnt to skate backwards though, no matter how she tried and she always favoured her right leg to steady herself while the left was always slightly raised. Why didn't Hamilton have a roller-skating rink like the ones she saw on the telly? She loved the graceful elegance of their fluid movements and poor Voula day-dreamed of becoming a famous figure skater one day, while her brothers wanted to be Essendon footballers.

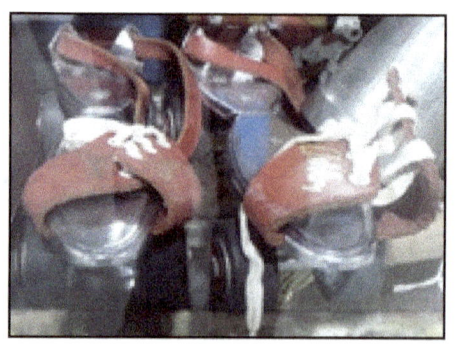

17 Byron Street, Hamilton, Victoria is an Edwardian style house built between 1900 and 1915. The pruned tree in front of the window on the left is still the same pink camellia tree of the 1960s! (2014)

Chapter 28
The First School Day Every Year

Every year during the holidays, Argyro would buy fabric from Millers. That store supplied all the different school uniform materials of the various schools round about Hamilton. Mothers would come in, buy a few yards of fabric, and make their sons' and daughters' summer uniforms. The Mothers' Club also offered to sew uniforms for a cheap price too, if desired. However, Argyro used her seamstress skills to make Voula's new school dresses and the boys' shorts, so at the start of every year, Voula went to school in a new, freshly starched frock and Peter and Jimmy sported new shorts. In those days, women had to sew their own clothes or employ someone else to make them. Yes you could buy off the rack, as we do nowadays, but it was quite expensive and if you wanted a perfect fit you had to pay to your clothes adjusted, so Argyro's skills were highly valued by the Hadis family too. Jumpers were usually hand-knitted so they were very pricey. Luckily Argyro could also knit!

It was always exciting starting the new school year: the children felt excited and elated to be in a higher class level. Before the summer holidays of the previous year they had visited their new teacher and classroom to familiarise themselves with the differences. The children were always excited to visit their new teacher and felt they had grown up a little bit more.

When Voula started grade five, Miss Slater handed out exercise books for the various subjects. The children carefully wrote their names on their belongings and put them into their desks. At home time, they took them home for their mothers to cover them with brown paper, to protect them from damage, as the exercise books had to last a whole year! The double desks seated two pupils and had lift-up lids so they kept all their books, rulers and writing materials in their desks. For special art and craft lessons, their teacher would give out coloured squares of paper. The paper smelt fresh and the pupils loved to sniff the new paper.

One day Miss Slater gave out three pieces of fresh, coloured squares, with strict instructions not to do anything with the paper until she gave permission, as it was expensive and not to be wasted by mistakes. She gave out scissors and showed the class how to cut two squares into strips of a particular measured width, using rulers. Next she asked the children to come to her desk, one at a time, with their third coloured sheet. At her desk she used a Stanley knife to cut rows of lines on their sheets. Finally she instructed the class on how to weave a pattern onto the sheet using the strips. There were many different variations and the woven paper served to teach about the art of weaving, and to learn names like *waft* and *warp*. Hamilton was the wool capital of Australia, so wool carding, sorting, spinning yarn and weaving were interesting facts for the children to learn.

Most children had their own set of pencils. Argyro would shave the ends of the pencils and write her children's names on them. Coloured sets of *Faber Castel* or *Derwent* were the most popular. Derwents were expensive but included silver and gold colours which were highly valued by the kids. When pupils were colouring-in, pencils were often borrowed by and loaned to classmates; especially gold and silver. So anyone who owned Derwents was guaranteed some popularity and influence in the class, at least during colouring and craft lessons. Voula also discovered a secret way of making her colours brighter and deeper, more permanent and more intense: she used to put water on the tips of the pencils and she kept the secret to herself too! Eventually the other kids figured it out though. Grade 5 was also the year students graduated from using an ink nib to gaining a "fountain pen licence," but only if their handwriting was considered up to scratch!

Blotting paper, water and ink were necessary items for penmanship and biro pens were not used until the middle of grade 6. The teachers thought that children's writing would "go to pot" if it wasn't carefully developed through the skills of writing with a nib, which required more care and concentrated effort.

Grade 5 was also the year Voula studied Social Studies, concerning other countries and their cultures as well as the Australian Explorers. Because she was the only child of migrant parents in the class, Voula was embarrassed, when one day Miss Slater asked her to tell the class what she ate for breakfast. Voula said porridge! Well it was a white lie because she was usually given toast, milk and an egg.

Grade 5 was an interesting year and the pupils felt important because, for the first time, they were allowed to use compasses, and templates of Australia and Victoria, to trace maps into their exercise books. These were bought from newsagents. There were little holes in the templates for the capital cities, so you could use a sharp pencil to make a dot there.

Another thing that they learned that year was to take turns recording weather readings. They measured air pressure and temperature from the barometer and rain levels using the water gauge.

That year, in order to raise money for charity, Miss Slater quietly entered a beauty pageant in the Hamilton Show. She blushed when the Headmaster, Mr Harris, announced her as the winner over the PA system. Observing this, the class unexpectedly became aware that teachers, although adults, may be vulnerable too, especially as she shyly explained to them that she had wanted to help raise funds for charity, and not that she felt herself to be beautiful! Anyhow, the class kids were proud of her because she was a caring and interesting teacher. They felt that the other grade 5 teacher was not as good as their teacher!

Jimmy and Voula are in their uniforms and on their way to school.

Chapter 29
Pleasures

Argyro loved posing for photos next to her cherished flowers and often insisted that her whole family do the same. It wasn't easy, as like many children, Jimmy, Peter and Voula were very impatient when it came to waiting for just the right photo to be taken by their long-suffering parent. Argyro would usually cut a nice long-stemmed flower and tell Voula to hold it (because she was a girl), while she took a photo with her old Box Brownie, held at waist level. One of her favourite places to visit was the Botanical Gardens, which presented seasonal displays of beautiful flowers. The children enjoyed the space of the Gardens where they could roll down grassy hills and play. In the early 1960s there was also a small zoo of caged guinea pigs, rabbits, cockatoos, budgerigars and monkeys. A couple of kangaroos and emus were also kept in a large enclosure. And there were peacocks too, often left to wander about. The ducks swam in a pond you could walk around, with an island in the middle for them to roost. Near the cages were some swings and a see-saw, and not far from the tall fountain was an old cannon you could sit on.

One day when the family travelled to Melbourne for a holiday to stay with Argyro's sister, Argyro wanted a photo of the event. The occasion also gave Argyro the opportunity to dress-up her only daughter with a hat. She put it on Voula's head and then wanted her to hold a lily, while her sister took a shot, but Voula wasn't happy at all. She wouldn't take the flower from her mother and Voula certainly hated wearing her hat! However, Argyro insisted it would look lovely to have a photo with flowers in the background and to hold a flower would enhance the memory, so she kept insisting. She was bitterly disappointed that her one and only daughter was not more obliging! Argyro's cajoling failed dismally with Voula and she decided her daughter was very disobedient and stubborn!

Argyro often wanted to take photos of her family in flower beds, even though the kids thought it was daggy and hated waiting around while their mother got the right shot. Of course Argyro wanted to take snap shots as keepsakes, to remember what life was like for her family, while her kids couldn't have cared less!

Even in her nineties Argyro loved her flowers and particularly her roses. Her favourite ones had a strong perfume, especially the red ones. No one seemed to have hay fever in those days, or maybe they didn't know much about it back then. She would cut them and put them in vases all over the house. Since their house had land all around it, Argyro had lots of space to grow flowers, as well as to make a big vegetable patch in her back yard. She grew tomatoes, spinach, pumpkin, beans, potatoes and silverbeet too. There was lots of parsley and mint too.

The fact that their house had land all around it came in handy too, because it was very accessible when Deidre visited. This girl was in Peter's grade, but she had also befriended Voula. Argyro gave permission for Deidre to bring her pet over when she visited. It was a horse! The kids took turns riding her horse around and around the house until Deidre thought it was time for her to go home.

There was another very special thing about Deidre: her home adjoined the local milk bar, for her parents were the proprietors.

Deidre being a kind girl, often had a bag of lollies to share with her friends. Voula's favourites were milk-bottles and raspberries, Peter's were bubble-gums because he liked the footie cards that came with them and Jimmy liked all lollies–he had a sweet tooth. (It may interest you to know that Jimmy grew up to become a dentist and he does advise his relatives not to eat sweets! Life is funny isn't it?) By the way, Voula's and Jimmy's favourite soft drink was Fanta while Peter's was Pepsi. Tasty soft drinks were made by the Tarax Company and were delivered in glass bottles in a crate, to the house. They used to have bottle caps on them and some people liked to collect all the different kinds of caps, as a hobby. Although diminished, it seems that Tarax is still available in some supermarkets.

From a young age, the children loved climbing all the fruit trees in the back yard. There was a shortish old apple tree and several different plum trees. The apple tree had a horizontal branch that they thought looked like a horse, so they tied a rope to it and bounced on the branch, pretending to ride it. That was fun until it broke under their weight and their mother was upset that the branch would not bear any more apples. Argyro told her children they should take better care of their trees, so they would get fruit from them. They each took responsibility for a tree and soon chose which trees belonged to whom. Peter wanted the tallest plum tree, near the back fence from which he had hung the "monorail". It had small yellow plums. Jimmy got the thick tree with the biggest and reddest plums as he found it easiest to climb and own as his. This was the tree around which they tied Voula, one of the times she was the Indian, when they played *Cowboys and Indians*. They left her there at lunchtime when their mother called them to come inside –but that's another story.

Voula had the plum tree with the medium-sized, red plums next to the swing and along the side fence. This tree had a branch growing almost horizontally across its trunk, at about two and a half metres from the ground. Voula could climb onto the crossbar of the swing, get onto the top horizontal beam of the paling fence and then onto the tree. However it was very uncomfortable because her shoes couldn't both fit in the angle of the branches. It was hard to stand there admiring the views of the neighbouring yards with only one shoe wedged sideways on a tree while the other had no foothold except two metres away.

Voula decided she should build a tree-house in her tree but lacked the skills. Argyro took pity on her and nailed a plank of timber on the tree, making a wonderful platform to stand on. The horizontal branch made a natural fence for Voula to lean on, which she held onto tightly because she was afraid of heights. Voula was ecstatic! She was often seen to climb gingerly onto her tree-house at dusk so she could watch the sun setting on the horizon. The colours of the sky provided infinite wonder and admiration of nature. She came to think of nature as her intimate friend and comforter during her times of solitude.

For her twelfth birthday the oldest Hadis kid, Theo, gave her a gift of some crystal gems he had bought, and also some that he had dug up. He enjoyed fossicking with his neighbour, a boy of about the same age. He was always studying and was older than all the kids. Theo also attended Hamilton College, one of the best private schools in Hamilton. He was considered too mature and studious to play with the younger children, because he was always in his bedroom reading. Theo Hadis grew up to became a lawyer and run his own business, so his diligence paid off!

One day she took the crystals up to her tree-house to admire them in the golden, glowing light of the setting sun and was instantly smitten by their sparkling light and colour. She decided to store them on her tree where she could enjoy them alone, at her favourite time of the day. Taking a rusty knife from the tool supply in the broken-down garage, she gouged out some little grooves in the surrounding branches and carefully placed her crystals into the grooves. There they remained for her pleasure and secret delight.

Every evening, just before dusk, it became a ritual to climb her tree, spy out the neighbouring yards for anything interesting going on, and then look towards the hills on the horizon. Have you noticed there is a special glow of golden light as the sun recedes and before the moon rises? During those few minutes, of the gloaming, when the golden sunlight shone on her gems, she would look at the effect on each individual crystal and relish the depth of beauty she beheld in each gemstone. They were all of various colours and sizes so they all sparkled differently. Being a bit fanciful, she pretended she was a princess and felt richer than a king in her tree-house palace! In the end though, Voula did *not* keep her crystals, but more of that later.

Another memory of Hamilton was a celebration called *Yulunga*, an Aboriginal word for "dance". Crowds gathered along Gray Street, outside Lucas Cafe, to watch the Yulunga parade. There were clowns, people on stilts, jugglers, floats and music bands marching by. It was fun, colourful and interesting. Everyone, helped; even the kids who would decorate their bikes and ride them in the parade. One year Peter and Bob put streamers through their bike spokes. Their bikes looked wonderful as they slowly rode them along in the parade. Jimmy and Voula cheered like mad for their brother, who had spent ages cleaning and decorating his beloved blue bike.

Here is a sample of Argyro's outdoor photos, with (of course) flowers in the background. Jimmy is in his school uniform.

From top right: the Botanical Gardens fountain; the canon; Voula hates her hat!

Chapter 30
The Club

Disneyland was the brainwave of Walt Disney in the mid1950s and it was an exciting new concept and very popular, because it captured everyone's imagination. There was Fantasy Land, Tomorrow Land and Adventure Land. In the 1960s, on Saturday evenings at 6:30pm, on Channel 7, *Walt Disney's Wonderful World of Colour* was never missed by anyone; it was extremely popular. Voula and her siblings came running when they heard the theme song, "When I wish upon a star".

They loved watching Disney movies and Mickey Mouse and his friends were popular too. There was even a Mickey Mouse Club in the United States! Watching Disney movies was the start of Voula's love of movies and sharing in great adventures. The three younger Hadis kids, along with Jimmy, Voula and Peter sometimes watched together, but most of the time they didn't watch TV because they were too busy doing things. It was on Disneyland's *Tomorrow Land* that Peter was first introduced to, and enthralled by, a monorail, and built his own monorail from his broken billy-cart.

One day, on TV, they saw something about the *Scouts, Girl Guides* and *Brownies* and it made them wish they could be in a club like that too. Of course some of their school friends were boy scouts and brownies, but Argyro and Theo were not comfortable about their kids getting involved in Aussie clubs, because of the cultural differences. They didn't know it was begun by Christian churches to help children develop upright morals and experience the outdoors, especially those children who had lost fathers during WW2. Also in those days, parents concentrated on work and many did not regard extra-curricular activities as very important at all, unless it was learning a musical instrument. Clubs and sports were just something kids did to occupy themselves and it was considered play-time. Consequently, Argyro and Theo never attended any of Voula's netball games on Saturday mornings, or any of Peter's footy matches; not many parents did, as they were mostly working or resting. Anyway, the seven children were together one day when Voula suggested how nice it would be to form a club, and that's just what they did!

Everyone had to contribute 5 cents to become a member and the money would go into the club's kitty. After some arguing they decided Jimmy and John were too young to have any money and that they could be members for free. Here is a little history and explanation about the club.

1. Voula wanted to call it the "Peacock Club", as there were some beautiful peacock feathers in the room, that Argyro had collected from the Botanical Gardens. But she had to negotiate, because the boys didn't like her bossy leadership and decided not to be members.

2. Voula realised the club would not even get off the ground, unless she had their support, so she told them it would be *their* club, asked Steven Hadis to be the president, and asked them for club name suggestions.

3. They voted, and as the boys had the numbers, they finally decided on the "PRINCE and PEACOCK CLUB". Everyone wanted to honour Prince, the family dog. Voula insisted on the J for "justice" as she could see rules would be needed and she

wanted the boys to be peaceable. To motivate them and to show them that the club really was theirs, Voula included the logo comprising of the letters: J for "justice", P for "Prince", and another P for "peacock".

4. Still they weren't very interested until she told them the club, not only offered a *library* for members, but it could buy *lollies* for them and also *lend them money* from the kitty! Steven borrowed 2 cents straight away and one can understand why Voula introduced the "oath of loyalty", seeing that his heart was fixed on financial matters and cupidity rather than in the joys of being a club member!

5. Rules included "no violence at meetings" due to the boys always arguing and fighting with her. As is evident, children can learn a lot about politics and diplomacy when they form a club!

Every club needs a constitution, so an exercise book was decorated by the Secretary, Voula, with some pink lolly foil and some silver chocolate foil, because it was shiny and she thought it looked classy. The words were a bit squashy though as there was not much room or forward planning of the layout. She did her best.

Written on the pink foil were the words: "J.P.P CLUB MONDAY 6th. 1. 69"

On the silver foil were the words: "PEACOCK JPP CLUB" and the club's logo followed by the secretary's initials, in an effort to make the book look more official. Of course every good club has rules and an oath, which in this case were:

"SILVER RULES

No Violence at Meetings" (Peter was sometimes prone to puerility and fisticuffs!)

"Kindness and respect to elders"   (Voula was the eldest!)

"OATH

We hereby swear to abide by the rules and be forever loyal or pay the consequences   (No consequences were stipulated; merely the threat of them!)

MOTTO

LIVE & DIE KNOWN BY GOODNESS WITHOUT SLANDER"

(Sometimes the boys stooped to character assassination!)

Before computers, library books had little pockets inside the back cover, with the details of the book written on a slip of cardboard placed inside. Voula busily stuck pockets and slips of paper into the back of each book she and her brothers owned, and also made a pocket in the club book for each member. She entitled the page "Library Roll" in her fanciest writing. The library was now open for business and late returns would probably be fined and the money go into the kitty, *if* everyone co-operated and obeyed the rules, just like for all libraries. The club was now officially begun and it was 6th January 1969!

In order to build up funds for the club, the kids decided to knock on the doors of houses around the block, and ask if anyone needed any small jobs done for a small payment of 10 or 20 cents. It was a bit scary, so they asked Argyro if she could come with them, but she said it would be better for the kids to go all together for safety, and that people would be kinder to kids rather than to adults. Well they knocked on quite a few doors, but either no one answered, or they didn't want anything done "at the moment".

At the last house, at the corner of the block, Voula knocked without much hope in her heart. She smiled politely at the prim lady who answered the door. The lady looked unimpressed that a bunch of hot-looking children were in her front yard, and she frowned at Voula. "Why are you knocking on my front door? It's rude!" she spoke like a teacher. "You are not visitors, so the right thing to do is to knock on my side or back door, like the trades people." Voula was shocked. She had heard of this sort of thing before, but had never expected that she would be considered rude, as this lady plainly seemed to think.

Voula was crestfallen and apologised. As she turned to leave the lady called after her and asked why she had come to her door. Voula replied that they were trying to raise some money for their club, by doing little jobs around the block. The lady thought for a moment and then, to the surprise of the boys, she asked if they knew how to mow her lawn with her hand-mower. Peter and Steve Hadis jumped at the opportunity, saying they often mowed for their parents (this was quite true). The lady led them to the garage and they returned with her mower. It was hard work but the ground was level and she had promised them 20 cents each!

While they were waiting, the girls and little boys did some weeding for free, to prove their bona fides and good will. They wanted to build a good reputation with their clients. When they became tired they went home, but the boys were still mowing; taking turns. However, it cannot be recalled what the club bought with the proceeds. Probably it was chocolates or lollies, as promised when the club was formed. After this the children found it difficult to find more jobs and their kitty funds dried up. As happens in the real world, their business also dried up with their funds! Soon after that, interest in the club, unfortunately, petered out and no other ideas for clubs ever managed to get off the ground!

Voula tried to retrieve the books the kids had borrowed, at the time the library was first formed. After that, she "borrowed" her own books and lent some to Peggy occasionally; that was all. Poor Voula felt a bit foolish and it had all been a lot of effort, However, it had been fun while it lasted, but also stressful trying to keep everyone interested. It was amazing that adults could keep their clubs going for years and years!

Chapter 31
The Sleepover

It was 1968 and it was a sad and sombre time for Voula when she finished grade six at Gray Street State School. It had been her first, and only school. She had attended it for most of her life, and it was where she came into contact with Aussies and their culture. In fact it had been a crucible, welding together the pervading, parochial country Australian culture of the 1960s, when assimilation was the go, with what her Greek parents had taught her of their culture and principles. She remembered the happy times of playing and being included in girl games, but Voula also realised she needed to make more of an effort to make friends with others outside her Greek culture. She thought about it for weeks and finally made a pact with herself: she would try to make friends with other girls, try to be popular. Somewhere she had heard: "If you want to have friends, then you have to be friendly". Yes! She would have a new start in high school, so she would try to fit in more, to be accepted by Aussies and not be seen as different from them. This was her serious promise to herself and an undertaking she would strive for: her New Year's Resolution. She told no one about her plan to become popular with her peers.

With the beginning of 1969, Argyro, as usual made Voula's new school dress, but bought the rest of her uniform: a dark green, felt Bowler hat and a matching wool-blend jacket. The jacket and hat also had badges pinned on the front of them, with the school motto: "I shall attain". When the time came to start Hamilton High, Voula was terribly excited. The teachers and buildings were unfamiliar and numerous too. This was the *big time*! It took a lot of getting used to. She felt so grown up and noticed how the teachers treated the students with respect.

One of her most favourite classes was French, and because she was fluent in Greek, thanks to the determined efforts of Argyro, who insisted on giving her lessons, Voula found it easy to learn a third language. They do say that if you know a couple of languages, it is easier to learn a third and a fourth one. However, maybe it was the new method the French teacher used. This teacher determined to utilise a new technique: the *audio-visual method*. This consisted of students listening to an audio of phrases while looking at pictures. No writing was read until the audio was repeated and properly pronounced several times. After that, students were allowed to read what they had been practising how to say. The teacher thought this would help her students to have better pronunciation without interference from the written words. In any case, it worked well for Voula as she consistently achieved the highest marks for her tests, in the class.

Another favourite subject was science, because of the science laboratories. It was fun to use *Bunsen Burners* and t*ripods, Florence flasks, test tubes, clasps* and *cylinders*. She learned a new genre of writing too, that of "scientific experiments". The exercise books were specially constructed for science diagrams and writing, having a blank page and a lined page side by side.

A further difference from primary school was that she was allocated a school locker for the year. Each student was to use it for their books, sports uniforms and school bags. Students were encouraged to buy a chain for their locker key that could be attached to a button on their jacket, while the key was deposited safely in a jacket pocket. Argyro felt proud of her "school children" and took a photo of them in their new uniforms; of course posing in front of her roses. (The key chain is visible on Voula's jacket.)

Voula concentrated, not only on her studies, but also on keeping the promise to herself, of making new friends. She tried to help others and be kind to them and it paid off: they voted her class captain and she was well-liked by her classmates. She was contented that finally she was no longer an outsider, or was she no longer an outsider because she was contented?

The fruition of being popular was that something happened that scared her a bit. Janine, a friendly girl in her class, invited her to spend the weekend at her place. Voula had never been invited for a sleepover before, and wasn't sure how her parents would react. Also, it was unknown territory for her: how would she cope living with a family of Scottish ancestry, away from her own family for two nights?

After discussing it with Voula, Argyro and Theo made an unexpected decision: she could go to Janine's home for the weekend. Consequently, after school on Friday, Janine's dad picked up the girls and drove them to his property. It was a sheep farm and quite a large spread. Everything seemed lovely, but the family were very reserved and her parents didn't speak much once the formalities were over. To make matters more uncomfortable, Voula found that she had to share a bed with Janine, which is something she wasn't used to. To add to this, apparently her friend was in the habit of not wearing underwear under her nightie! This seemed most peculiar to Voula and she lost her vivaciousness, becoming quiet and nervous. On Saturday the girls killed time walking around the farm and looking at the flocks and feeding the orphaned lambs, but Voula was homesick. Janine asked what was wrong but Voula only replied that everything was good.

After another uncomfortable and sleepless night, Voula tried to be outgoing and friendly, but with limited success and felt relieved when she was finally driven home on Sunday afternoon. On Monday, at school, lining up outside a classroom and waiting for the teacher to arrive, the girls' eyes met. After initial greetings Janine turned away and spoke to another girl. Janine wasn't very sociable anymore and found a new best friend to hang around with. Well that suited Voula just fine! All the same it was a disappointing ending and she hoped Janine wouldn't malign her name with possible negative gossip. One thing for sure: no more sleep-overs for her!

Chapter 32
New Beginnings

No one could believe it: a man was going to walk on the moon! It was Monday 21st July 1969, and Voula was attending classes at Hamilton High School. That day the principal of the school had arranged groups of students to go to nearby homes of students who had televisions. So at the beginning of lunchtime, Voula and some other students, from different class levels, walked to a schoolmate's house around the corner from the school to watch the live telecast of Neil Armstrong taking his first steps on the moon.

Everyone was very enthused to witness this historic event, but to tell you the truth Voula found it difficult to make sense of the TV images for two reasons. Firstly, everything was in black and white and secondly, there was a lot of interference and static. Furthermore, even the speaking of the astronauts was unclear. Anyway it was still a momentous occasion and everyone waited to watch it all happen. Then, at 12.56 Eastern Standard Time, Neil Armstrong stepped off the lunar module ladder and put his footprint in the moon dust. His now famous words were spoken, "That's one small step for (a) man, one giant leap for mankind".

Theo was cynical and did not believe that it had actually happened. For many years he was of the opinion it had all been a fabrication, so that NASA could go on spending money on space travel. Moreover, he was not the only one, because many people still hold to this conspiracy theory. Since that time much more evidence has been collated and there appears little doubt that Apollo 11 did, in fact, land on the moon.

Some scientists thought that there would be a lot more moon dust on the surface of the moon, because the *Theory of Evolution* states that the moon is millions of years old. However Mr Armstrong did not sink deeply into the dust, but left a neat footprint a few centimetres deep, proving the moon to be far younger than anticipated. Nevertheless, he was a very brave man.

At this time, during the Cold War, the world was anxious that either the president of the USSR or the president of the USA would "press the red button" and "nuke" the world. Everyone was afraid that if this happened, a nuclear war would mean the end of the world. A nuclear disaster was considered a real, daily, nefarious possibility. Ever since 1962, and the averted Cuban Missile Crisis, the world was on tenterhooks! There was an open contest between the Soviet Union and the USA, as to who would be the first to land and walk on the moon. Now of course, the west was congratulating itself, but Armstrong, with his word of "mankind" united all human hearts regardless of race or nationality.

Humanity saw pictures of the Earth from the moon for the first time, and everyone appreciated how small, yet unique our planet really is. Accordingly, the popular school atlas, *Robinson's Primary World Atlas*, was replaced in popularity by the *Jacaranda Atlas*, mainly because it displayed some beautiful colour photos of the Earth taken from the moon. Everyone was amazed!

Voula too, along with her classmates, comprehended the beauty and preciousness of our planet. "We must take good care of it," she thought. It was the topic of that time, because people started to seriously and publicly consider looking after our planet. The thought of being custodians of the Earth and of protecting it for future generations began organisations like *Greenpeace*, which formed in 1971. In Australia the litter on our roadsides was atrocious and the *Keep Australia Beautiful* campaign really took off in the same year.

During this time new movements were born against pollution and keeping the planet "green". Australia was the first country to have a "green" political party: the *Australian Greens* came out of the *United Tasmania Group* set-up to fight against the attempt to dam the Franklin River in 1972. Now, The Greens are part of the Australian political landscape. Things were changing in Australia and in Hamilton too. Lucas Cafe, affected by the new counter lunches offered to hotel customers, was closing its doors.

Theo and Argyro were thinking about moving, as they had concerns of their own: they were mindful that their children would probably leave home to get a tertiary education, as Hamilton did not have any local universities. Education was highly regarded and many children went to boarding schools, for their secondary education, and even Bob Tydon boarded during the week and came home on weekends. He would eventually leave for Melbourne to study law at Melbourne University.

All this concerned Theo and furthermore, jobs were scarce, so where would their children find work? Therefore, like many families whose children had outgrown the town, they "bit the bullet" and decided to move to the city–Melbourne.

Theo's and Andy's business partnership ended after fifteen years, when they told their landlord that they did not want to renew their lease. No one bought Lucas Cafe; it simply closed its doors. Then the Hadises moved to Adelaide where Andy's wife had a brother, and Theo took his family to Melbourne, where Argyro had two sisters and a brother. Their Melbourne house had a bus stop right outside, and noisy traffic was ongoing day and night. Voula was too shy to roller blade on the footpath, and Argyro forbad her children to ride their bikes, as she thought the streets were too dangerous for them to go cycling. A year later, Prince, their pet dog, met his demise on busy Bell Street. After escaping through a hole in the back fence he chased another dog through the furious traffic and he was hit by a car. Argyro and Voula had run after him and saw it happen. They were heart-broken and Argyro wept on Voula's shoulder. They wished then that the family had stayed in Hamilton!

Voula had been heart-broken to leave her beloved Hamilton! So many memories would be left behind! On the final morning she went out to look down Billy Goat Hill, as everything sparkled silver and clean in the morning light. Even the power lines were decorated with diamond dew drops, each perfectly formed and wonderful. As she etched the view from the top of the Hill into her memory, she told herself with determination never to forget the charming scene before her. The balanced symmetry and serene beauty of the spires belonging to the two churches in the distance, surrounded by trees and houses, were to her mind better than any other in the entire world. What a romantic! It was time to leave; it was time to grow up, but still the heart retains a strong attachment and yearning for home, the place of one's birth.

On the last evening before their departure, Voula climbed onto the single timber plank of her tree-house. She wanted just one last time to admire the view and her sparkling gemstones, glittering in the golden light of the gloaming. You remember, she had notched her best crystal gems into the branches of her tree-house, as decorations. Now she resolved to leave them there, in the branches. They should stay where they belonged. It was her tribute and a seemly sacrifice of value, to her special place, which she had grown to love.

When the family left for Melbourne it was September 1969. Voula suspected her childhood was over. "I'll be back one day!" she promised herself. In fact it would be about thirty years before she would re-enter Hamilton and be recognised by her old neighbour Don Shmitz, who remembered the tones of her voice!

Voula was a month off her 13th birthday and just at the present she didn't want to live in the city! What would it be like? At least there would be more people of different nationalities there, and Melbourne had the world's third largest Greek population in the world. However, she didn't like changes in her life and this was a significant upheaval! What also plagued her mind was she was also unsure she would enjoy becoming a teenager, after the debacle with Katie! And how did her brothers feel about the move? Peter didn't really want to leave his mate, Bob, but was stoic about it, and Bob paid a visit to the family a few years later during a term break from his uni studies. Jimmy, being nearly nine didn't seem to mind too much one way or the other. As for Argyro and Theo, they were quite delighted to have been fortunate enough to purchase a house across the road from Argyro's married sister, in Preston!

In any case, it was the end of country life and a new era in Melbourne was about to begin for the family. Jimmy's, Peter's and Voula's childhood home would be left behind, but isn't that so for many of us? Isn't it true that life is full of final chapters and new beginnings? Perhaps how we live and interact with others has more bearing on us than where we live.

Finally, dear reader, thank you for taking the time to share in my childhood memories and to take a walk in my skin. It has been confusing at times to recollect childhood experiences with the reasoning of an adult. I have tried not to alter the facts and the ideas of the child, but no doubt the puerility of the child has been influenced and tempered by the understanding of the adult.

Alas, now our journey together has come to an end. Fare thee well on *your* life's journey and let us take leave of each other with a portion of an old Irish prayer:

> Let us be thankful for life,
> and for time's olden memories
> that are good and sweet.
> And may the evening's twilight
> find you gentle still.
>
> May your day be touched
> by God's blessings,
> brightened by a song in your heart,
> and warmed by the smiles
> of the people you love.
>
> *anonymous*

original facade of Hamilton High (now Brambridge College)

the view from Billy Goat Hill with the two church spires (2014)